Healing, Heartache and Humour

From Rejection of God to Seeing His Astounding Power

Steve Morgan

ISBN: 978-1-907929-90-8

All Scripture quotations are taken from the New International Version unless otherwise stated. Copyright © 1973, 1978 International Bible Society. Published by Hodder and Stoughton.

Steve Morgan can be contacted at: steve.morgan8@icloud.com
Website: http//stevemorgan8.co.uk
Twitter @smorgan842

Ip

Editing, design and layout by Life Publications
www.lifepublications.org.uk

Dedication

I would like to dedicate this book to my wife Sian
and my late wife Marilyn.
Their faith and love have made the writing of this
book possible.

Healing, Heartache and Humour

Commendations

Steve is a devoted lover of Jesus Christ, who has consistently sought to bring the Good News to all those apparently unpromising places where Jesus Himself longs to be met and heard. I have had the joy of seeing at first hand something of the ministry he has exercised, and this lively, moving book, which paints an honest picture of faith in hard times as well as times of manifest blessing, is a real gift to God's people. It witnesses to the fact that God's active presence among us is as powerful and transforming as it ever was. It will stir and nourish faith.

The Most Reverend Dr Rowan Williams
(Former Archbishop of the Church in Wales
and retired Archbishop of the Church of England)

My wife and I were members of Steve's congregation at Christchurch, Merthyr Tydfil, for more than twenty years. This book is a pleasure to read, easy and accessible. It does what it says on the tin. It can be read in one sitting or dipped into like a bag of sweets. Each selection will deliver what is promised. He tells us that another book with the theological background to his experiences of God at work in his life and the lives of those he ministered with is in the pipeline. It will be a lovely complement to this volume.

Professor Jonathan Richards FRCGP
Visiting Professor of Primary Care, University of South Wales
Former General Practitioner

Steve Morgan has had a long, faithful and extraordinary ministry in the Diocese of Llandaff. His book brings out clearly his strong belief in the power and presence of God and of prayer; his willingness at all times to stand up for what he believes and his desire to reach out to those on the margins of society. And it is all written with considerable humour, humility and grace.

The Most Reverend Dr Barry Morgan
(Retired Archbishop of the Church in Wales)

Having known Steve for many years, the warmth, wisdom and insight with which he delivers his story in *Healing, Heartache and Humour* is no surprise to me. Breath-taking stories of miraculous healing, deliverance from evil and lives transformed by Jesus are as formational to his journey as the heartache of bereavement and rejection. I felt privileged and enriched just to peer through this window onto Steve's remarkable life so far.

Reverend Elfed Godding
National Director, Evangelical Alliance Wales

Contents

Foreword

During nineteen years leading the Evangelical Alliance in Wales I have enjoyed the privilege of walking with some outstanding Christians. Canon Steve Morgan is one of them.

On one occasion, when Steve and I were enjoying a coffee and catch-up he shared with me his idea of writing a Training Manual for the Church's ministry of healing. Knowing his remarkable life of faith and healing I responded by asking him "Why don't you write your autobiography first?" I am so glad he agreed because I know the impact the book will have on ministers, church members and the wider population of Wales and beyond. I will explain why.

Steve's vivid description of his own pilgrimage in *Healing, Heartache and Humour* provides a porthole into a life that has surfed the peaks of joy and embraced the troughs of pain with equal faith in God and deep trust in His love and grace.

Rarely do I oscillate between laughter and tears as frequently but in reading this book I had reason to do so. The honesty with which Steve draws us into the exhilaration and anguish of his story is reminiscent of the psalmists, the worshippers of God who loved Him enough to express their hurt as well as their adoration.

Having known Steve for many years, the warmth, wisdom and insight with which he delivers his story is no surprise to me. Breath-taking accounts of miraculous healing, deliverance from evil and lives transformed by Jesus are as formational to his journey as the heartache of bereavement and rejection.

It is noteworthy too that Steve has waited until this point in his life to reveal his story, enriched by the passage of time, honed by biblical insight and reflection, tested and proved worthy of telling. The joys and pains of Steve's journey are woven into the text providing a rich three-dimensional life perspective.

I am struck by Steve's tenacity. He has stood by his calling to serve in the Church in Wales as an evangelical minister; a man committed to the proclamation of the Gospel, the authority of scripture and the use of charismata to build the church (1 Corinthians 14:12) while graciously engaging with some colleagues who hold a different conviction. There are occasions when he could have thrown in the towel, but he has pursued his calling.

There are many things that I have learned from Steve; he has a raw passion to reach with the Good News of Jesus Christ those who are on the margins of our societies, in the wake of an approach to church that sometimes militates against this goal. He has preferred to reach the lost with the love of Jesus rather than achieving some of the accolades and honours bestowed upon long-serving ministers.

A man of deep conviction of the importance of serving in the power of the Holy Spirit, Steve has unashamedly crossed boundaries that some of us may resist. He has seen the power of God triumph over the demonic and heal the terminally sick. Equally commendably he has maintained his faith when the Lord has called a parishioner home to heaven rather than healing their illness.

Steve is a Welshman serving in his beloved Wales. A man who believes that the Gospel of Jesus Christ that has catalyzed more revivals in Wales than in the other UK nations can transform his nation once again. He has never given up; never opted for easier parishes, never doubted he is in the right place.

I will be amazed if this book fails to inspire, challenge and spur you on in your pursuit of effective mission.

Reverend Elfed Godding
Baptist Minister
National Director of Evangelical Alliance Wales 1999-2018

1

My Conversion Experience

At 9.15am on Friday October 21, 1966, over 150,000 cubic metres of water-saturated mining debris broke away from tip No. 7 at Aberfan. The landslide destroyed a farm, 20 terraced houses, and parts of Pantglas Junior and Senior school, killing 28 adults and 116 children.

As news of the Aberfan Disaster was being broadcast, I instantly blamed God and told him so in no uncertain terms. My instinct was to go there and offer to help, but the media put out a plea to dissuade people from going as the area was already inundated with so many onlookers that the rescue attempts were being hampered.

When I went to bed that night, I continued to blame God and felt an overwhelming sense of anger and uselessness. These feelings remained with me and my anger towards God grew into a bitterness as the weeks passed. I was not a Christian and could not understand why anybody would want to follow a God who could allow such a tragedy to take place.

Several weeks later, I awoke in the early hours of the morning in a bath of perspiration, and immediately felt a presence in the room. I was as confused as I was frightened. The awareness of the presence grew and I pulled the bedclothes over my head hoping it would subside and go away. But as the intensity of the presence grew, I threw the bedclothes off and leapt out of bed to confront what was in the room. I hastily looked around but didn't see anything that might account for the very real presence of something awesome in the bedroom. I took flight and made a beeline for the door to escape from whatever it was. I didn't make it. In the corner of room, by the door, appeared a small golden light about the size of a tennis ball. I was transfixed by the light and my fear ebbed away quickly. A calmness came over me as the light gradually grew in size. In the midst of the light there appeared the form of a man in a long white robe. Then I heard the word "Steve". The voice was so gentle and loving that I felt incredibly affirmed and wanted. It was as if every part of my being knew who it was who had said my name. All bodily strength left me as I sank to the floor. I cried out, "Oh God. Why me, after all I've said about you and all I've done? I don't understand."

For several minutes I just lay there on the floor, cupping my head in my hands, weeping and saying that I was sorry over and over again and pleading for forgiveness. Then, I very gingerly raised my head to look again at Jesus in the light, but the bedroom was all in darkness once more. My head slowly turned towards the bedroom window. We lived out in the countryside and I didn't always close my curtains. This night they were open. What happened next is very difficult to describe. It was as if I was transported above the earth and looking down at a vision of the suffering in the world. A variety of emotions seemed to cascade over me. Bereavement, despair, terror and depression took on visible forms as I looked at individuals and groups of people being overwhelmed by suffering. Then Jesus appeared in the midst of the chaos and He looked up at me and beckoned me with His hands to come down. My response was to cry out over and over again, "Yes Lord." The vision then left me and the next thing that I knew was waking up on the floor at the foot of the bed.

The night had gone and the morning had broken. I felt an overwhelming sense of peace that I had never known before. I felt clean on the inside for the first time. It was as if the Lord had given me a fresh start, a new beginning. A new dawn had come upon my life and I knew inwardly that I would never be the same again.

A great deal of time was spent reading the bible during the following days and weeks as I pondered and prayed what this amazing experience should mean for my life. At that time I was studying for my 'A' Levels, having secured a provisional place at Cardiff University to study Medicine. But my appetite for a medical career was waning and finally quashed completely when it was discovered that I was colour blind. My school applied to the Examining Board for a special dispensation as there was no way that I could pass the Chemistry Practical Examination without being able to do chemical titrations that involved noticing colour changes when liquids were mixed together. The application was rejected. My hopes for a career in medicine were shattered. At the time my emotions oscillated from feeling crestfallen to that of a strange sense of release and peace.

I remember praying to the Lord that I would trust Him for my future as I felt that I could not put my trust in any decision that I had made prior to my conversion experience. Some said that I was irresponsible as I told people I was going to fail my 'A' Levels deliberately because I would not need them for the future that the Lord had for me. They may have been right, but I felt I needed to make a declaration of trust in the Lord. In all my prayers and bible reading, the Lord had been silent as to what He wanted for me, but I knew that I knew that He had called me to something that would involve engaging with suffering people. For a while it seemed as if my life was on hold. It was as if someone had pressed a pause button, and in this state of limbo a peace came over me that was both encouraging and reassuring.

2

My Call to Ordination

After my conversion experience, I began to attend several local churches in search of a spiritual home where I would be able to settle down and receive both insight and guidance. Some of the churches that I visited left me spiritually confused. I went in as a stranger and came out as a stranger. In my naïvety I thought I would be meeting some of the happiest people on earth, but actually found them to be unwelcoming and unhelpful. Not one of them asked me if I would be returning – perhaps it was just as well! However, when I attended the local Anglican church of St Peter's in Dinas Powis, the contrast from my previous experiences could not have been greater.

I was welcomed at the door as a guest and taken straight away to be introduced to the Rector of the parish, the Rev John Lloyd Richards. He was perfectly charming and I instantly perceived that he was a man of God. He called a church member to sit with me and help me through the service. I thought this was an impressive example of the welcoming of a stranger and I immediately sensed I had at last found a spiritual home. The service was fully liturgical and seemed to be packed with phrases that I did not understand. However, although the phraseology of the liturgy alienated me from being able to engage fully, I was aware of a profound sense of spiritual hunger for further discovery. After the service, I spoke again with the Rector and he invited me to his home to hear my story.

John proved to be a great help to me at this time. I began attending his church regularly and felt very comfortable in his presence as someone who had a very real relationship with the Jesus whom I was becoming to know. I appreciated the time he gave to me and the wisdom of his words. Indeed, when I joined his Confirmation class, he showed great composure and grace at the barrage of questions that came his way from this recent convert. I had an insatiable appetite, not only for more knowledge, but for prayer guidance so I would not only get to know more about Jesus and my new found faith, but also discover how to develop a deeper personal relationship with my Lord.

When I asked John if he had anything to say that might help me understand the implications of what I had experienced at my conversion, he was very guarded. When I challenged him about this, he said he was convinced that the Lord would let me know when the time was right and when I was ready. This didn't help me a great deal at the time and I expressed my impatience. He said I would have to learn the lesson of being content with periods of silence from the Lord, and I needed to trust Him and believe they were times of challenge to spiritual growth and not an indication of indifference from the Lord. John gave me additional books to read, but equally as important, he gave me his time. I coveted my time with him and was so appreciative of his deep spirituality. This was especially needed when I returned from a conference at Coleg Y Fro in Rhoose, South Wales. John had encouraged me to broaden my horizons and seek other contexts in which I could grow further in my faith.

The conference considered "The Church in the 60s" and I was hungry to discover more about the Church, the bible, and what the Lord had in store for me. At the end of the conference, the chairman, the Rev Alun Davies, invited any questions or comments from the participants. Frustration got the better of me as I felt I had not received any further direction from the Lord during the conference. Consequently I was quite rude and said sarcastically that I now believed in miracles more than I had ever believed in them before. He ingratiated himself and I quickly added that I believed it was a miracle that anybody went to the kind of church that the conference had described. There was a stunned silence as I sat down in anger. I surprised myself at this public show of frustration as I was by nature, quite introverted. It seemed to me that another opportunity had proved abortive in my quest to discover the meaning and purpose of my conversion experience.

As the chairman fielded other questions and comments, I noticed he had written a note and passed it to one of the speakers. He then in turn, came to me and handed me the note. It read, "Come and see me after the end of the conference". I thought, "Right, now I am going to give him both barrels". It never happened. I didn't get the chance to vent my anger. Instead, he totally disarmed me. After the conference had ended, I was ushered to a small room and invited to sit down. The first question he asked me was, "What have you got against God?" I replied that I had nothing against God, but was desperate to understand what my conversion experience meant for me. He then asked me if I would tell him my story of coming to faith.

I explained to him that prior to my conversion experience, all was going well with my life. I was getting on well with my 'A' levels in Biology, Chemistry and Physics and had a provisional place at Cardiff University to study Medicine. However, after my conversion experience, I lost all interest in becoming a doctor. I interpreted this to mean that the Lord did not want me to become a doctor as He had something different for me to do. Then, as if to confirm this, I had the bombshell of discovering that I was colour blind. I told him that my biology teacher brought into the class a colour supplement from *The Sunday Telegraph* with a colour blind test. There were four pictures that were composed of different coloured dots. If someone was colour blind then that person would see four very different pictures from those seen by someone who was not colour blind. Sitting next to me in the class was a pupil named Grant. He was known to be colour blind, so the teacher asked him if he would do the test. He agreed and then went through the pictures and proceeded to describe what he could see.

I retorted that the test was rubbish because I saw exactly what Grant saw. The teacher then rounded on me and said that I was colour blind as well. I did not believe him until he asked other pupils if they would do the test. They all saw very different pictures to the ones that Grant and I saw. Very quickly after this incident came the challenge in Chemistry and I realised I would never be able to pass my Chemistry Practical Examination. My heart sank and I wallowed for a while in failure and self-pity. But then, when I spent some time to be alone and consider this news, I resolved that I was going to deliberately fail my 'A' levels and throw myself completely on the Lord's mercy and guidance. This may have been naïve and immature, but it was who I was at the time and it did give me a great measure of peace. I explained that having laid down all my previous aspirations, I was now struggling to find out what the Lord wanted me to do. He sat back in his chair and asked me to take my time and tell him more of my life story.

I began by telling him a little about my early childhood. I said I had struggled at school and had failed my '11 Plus' Exam, but instead of going to the local Secondary School, I was sent to Monkton House, a private school in Cardiff. I struggled there as well and for the first three years was near the bottom of the class. Indeed, I remember a teaching telling me, "Morgan, you are as thick as two short planks, and that is an insult to the two short planks."

In the year prior to sitting the private school's 'O' level equivalents, I had an average mark of 22 per cent in my exams. Then, when it came to picking subjects to be studied at the Senior College of Preceptors the following year, Scripture clashed with Physics. I wanted to do both. The school allowed me to do both, but I was told I would not be able to attend any of the Scripture lessons so did all the studying on my own at home. When it was time to sit the examinations, something remarkable happened. Scripture was the first exam. On the night before the exam, I was revising whilst sitting up in bed. Just before I put the light out, I prayed a very short prayer. I don't recall ever having prayed before so the prayer was short, blunt and to the point. It went like this, "God, I don't know if you are there or not but, if you are, then my first exam is about you. If you are there, I couldn't half do with some help. Could you help me push the pen in the right directions please?"

The prayer was trite, childlike, simple and as silly as that. In all honesty, I think the prayer was not one of any great conviction but one of desperation and pre-examination nerves. In any event, when it came time for the exam, I remembered the prayer I had prayed the night before and as I picked up the pen, I prayed, "Oh God, please help me to push the pen in the right directions". I turned over the question paper and began to write. My mind was racing and I soon got writer's cramp as I tried to keep up with the thoughts that came flooding to me. This was amazing. I had never known anything like this before. By the time the exam was finished, I was exhausted both mentally and physically. My mind was still buzzing with quotes from the Acts of the Apostles – one of the books of the bible that was part of the syllabus. However, by the evening, the euphoria had died down and I was now faced with the next exam. I thought that this experience of the Scripture exam was a freak, a one off, and had no expectation that it could ever happen again. Nevertheless, when I had finished my last minute revising for the two exams I had the next day, I thought, "Oh what the heck. It worked last time. I've got nothing to lose – I'll pray that prayer again". So I prayed that God would help me to remember what I had been taught and help me to push the pen in the right directions once again. The exams seemed to go quite well, and so I ended up praying a similar prayer each night before the remainder of the exams.

When the day came for the results of the exams to be published, unlike the other pupils in my class, I didn't get a letter from the school. It was now the summer school holidays and we had been told that the school would send the results by post. My mother contacted the school and the Secretary said the school had received my results but that they had queried them and returned them to the Examining Board for ratification. After a couple of weeks, my mother contacted the school again. They informed her that the Examining Board had confirmed the original results were correct, but that the school had once again queried the marks. There was another wait before the results finally arrived in the post. I was amazed. I had never before had such high marks. I even had distinctions. On returning to school for the Autumn term, I eagerly awaited the annual prize-giving at the Reardon Smith Lecture Theatre in Cardiff. When I compared my results with the rest of the class, I discovered I had the highest average mark overall; the highest mark for the Sciences, as well as the highest number of subjects passed because I had done Scripture on my own.

At the Prize Giving event I was excited about the prospect of going forward to receive my prizes as I had never won anything before in my life. The time came for the announcing of the winner for the highest average mark. I was puffed up with pride and sat on the edge of my seat as I got ready to make my way to the stage to receive my prize when the Headmaster said, "And the prize for the highest average mark goes to John Salter". I was crestfallen. The school had refused to accept my results and had discounted me from any prize whatsoever, even the prize for the highest number of subjects passed. The maximum number that could be taken was ten and because I had done Scripture on my own I had passed eleven – to no avail.

The following year, I passed all my 'O' levels and then left the school to go to Penarth Grammar School to study Biology, Chemistry and Physics at 'A' level. One of the consequences of my disappointment and anger at not receiving recognition from my school was that I never prayed again. I was angry at God, and felt totally disillusioned with everything to do with authority. As far as I was concerned, I was on my own and that was the way it was always going to be. I resolved to just get on with it and not expect any favours from anyone. Any thoughts of God disappeared in the vortex of self-pity, rejection and disappointment. That was why my conversion experience was totally unsolicited and unexpected.

When I had finished telling my story, Alun Davies then leant forward and asked me, "Do you think that God is calling you to Ordination?" I laughed out loud and retorted nervously, "No way. I believe many things about God now but I don't believe He is a fool".

I shudder now when I think of how immature and disrespectful was my response. He then began to speak my language for the first time and asked if I was prepared to put it to the test. I had always loved the sciences and the experimental tests of research (apart from titrations!). I immediately said, "Yes", and jumped at the opportunity. He said that he would make arrangements and would be in touch with me shortly. I was elated as I drove home. Someone, at last, was taking me seriously. Alun Davies had restored my faith in humanity. He had listened to my story and not taken offence at my immaturity and rudeness. It was as if he had seen through me and understood that my anger and sarcasm were outbursts of emotion that flowed from someone who was desperately struggling to find meaning and purpose in life.

True to his word, within a fortnight, he had spoken to Rev John Lloyd Richards, my Rector from Dinas Powis, and together they had arranged for me to have an interview with the Provincial Ordination Selection Panel of the Church in Wales. I was as nervous as a kitten as I sat in the waiting room with the other candidates. One by one the prospective Ordinands went in for their interviews which took about half an hour. When it was my turn, on entering the interview room, I was confronted with a veritable Sanhedrin of Church notables. I had barely sat down on a small wooden chair when the Chairman asked my why I wanted to be ordained. My reply was unrehearsed and I blurted out, "I don't want to be Ordained. It is the last thing that I want. I have had a life-changing experience and I need you to tell me if you think God is calling me towards Ordination". The members of the committee started an animated discussion amongst themselves after which the Chairman said, "We'll be in touch. Next please!"

That was it. My interview had lasted barely a few minutes. As I left the room, I felt dejected, let down and confused. It felt like a walk of shame as I slowly walked past the startled faces of the candidates in the waiting room. I felt sure that I had blown it and that 'being in touch' would simply be a letter to tell me I had not been successful. Failure, yet again, seemed to be the story of my life repeating itself.

Several days later, I received a letter inviting me to see the Rev Cledan Mears who was the Doctrine lecturer at St Michael's Theological College. He proved to be the person I was destined to meet in order to bring further clarity and understanding with regards to the call of God upon my life. After taking the time to hear my story, he then asked me several questions about the bible and my beliefs. His comment afterwards was, "You're a strange one". He went on to say that people who have experiences such as the one I had, either become extremely High Church or extremely Low Church. I confessed that I had no idea as to what those terms meant as I had only recently begun going to Church. He laughed and said I would find out soon enough. He confirmed he felt that I did indeed have a call upon my life for Ordination and he would recommend me to those in authority whose decision it would be to offer me a place at the college as an Ordinand. He did say there would have to be an unprecedented discussion about my situation because I had failed my 'A' levels. However, he felt confident that my eighteen 'O' levels and equivalents could go a long way in convincing the hierarchy in the Church and the University to make an exception in my case.

After a series of negotiations between the authorities at Cardiff University and St Michael's Theological College, I was offered a place at the college as an Ordinand and invited to study for a degree in Theology. I refused. I asked what was the minimal academic requirement in order to be Ordained. I was told it would be the Diploma in Theology course. I was determined to take the Diploma course and not the Degree course because, as I explained, I never wanted to 'get on' in the Church. My passion was to minister to people in the midst of their emotional and physical challenges. I was afraid I would not have the character to be able to resist any preferment that might come my way so I would rather choose to be one of the lesser lights amongst the clergy. It was not a case of denigrating anyone or denying the appropriateness of preferment as the Church encouraged and identified additional leadership qualities from amongst its clergy. It was simply a case of wanting to fully concentrate my energies on those who were members of the local Church and the community in which the Church served. I would not be dissuaded from my decision and the senior clerics in the department eventually relented and accepted me as a candidate on the Diploma Course.

Healing, Heartache and Humour

3

My College Days

And so in 1967 I went to St Michael's College in Llandaff to study for Ordination. As I nervously approached the door to the college, I wondered what I would encounter. I need not have been worried because I was met at the door by an Ordinand named David Yeoman. He asked to take my case and offered to show me to my room. He was charming and told me if ever I needed anything then all I had to do was to ask him and he would be there for me. He made me feel at home straight away and he was certainly true to his word. He later became an Assistant Bishop in the Diocese of Llandaff. This was indeed a well-deserved appointment and he became a much loved and well respected priest throughout the diocese.

In my first year at college, I felt out of my depth in the presence of so many Ordinands whose lives were steeped in both church attendance and responsibilities within the local churches from which they came. A number of them were the sons of priests and they brought a wealth of experience of church life. However, although I confessed to being a complete 'rookie' as a Christian, they did make me feel a part of this 'family' of Ordinands. Nevertheless, in the first year, I was not very sociable as I spent as much time as possible studying subjects that were all new to me.

I struggled with learning Greek but was energised by Philosophy. I felt a little guilty about my liking of Philosophy as I imagined it would be of little use in the practical work of being a priest. Yet it captivated my imagination. I even asked Professor Durrent, the Philosophy lecturer, if I could attempt to write a paper on proving the existence of God by developing the works of Anselm and Aquinas. He agreed, and after he read the paper, he told me that if I decided at any time to not go through with Ordination Training, then he would commend me to study Philosophy. Although he pointed out several flaws in my argumentation, he commended me for a germ of originality. The paper was no more than a collection of philosophical musings as I had no serious aspirations of being a philosopher.

Professor Durrent was a popular lecturer with the students. He would puff away on his pipe and re-light it several times with his box of matches. After a while, we decided we would take a guess as to how many matches he would get through in a lecture. At the end of a lecture we would be asked if we had any questions. It was easy to tell which students had guessed a higher number of matches than had been used as they began to ask questions so that he would re-light his pipe. It wasn't long before he cottoned to what we were doing, and with a wry smile at the end of one of his lectures he put his pipe in his pocket whilst slowly scanning the class of students and then, without saying a word, he left.

There were a number of occasions when the Doctrine lecturer, Cledan Mears, invited me back to his flat for further encouragement and advice. I don't know if I could have survived if it were not for his kindness. Much to my relief, I managed to pass all of my first year exams.

In the second year, I felt completely accepted and really began to settle in. The balance between studying and extra-curricular activities began to take shape with some controversial eccentricities. I joined the college football team. This was a source of great amusement and good exercise. I always looked forward to the times when Cledan Mears was the referee. Oftentimes, when a foul took place he would blow his whistle and say to the offender, "Hmm. I think that might have been a foul. What do you think?"

The highlight of the year was the annual match with the South Wales Baptist College. I wouldn't say that they were rough matches, but to a spectator it might have looked more like a contest as to how high can you kick a Baptist or an Anglican. There was one hilarious moment when I committed a foul and Cledan Mears said to me that I had committed a 'Rapture tackle'. I said that I didn't have a clue as to what that was. He said that that was because he had not lectured on it yet. After the match, I asked him what a 'Rupture tackle' was. I thought he had said 'rupture' as I had never heard the word 'Rapture' before. He laughed and told me to read 1 Thessalonians 4:13 to the end of the chapter. When I got back to the college and looked up the reference. I still did not understand, so I went to see him. He read from verse 16 to most of verse 17.

> *"For the Lord himself will come down from heaven, with a loud command, with the voice of the archangel and with the trumpet call of God, and the dead in Christ will rise first. After that, we who are still alive and are left will be caught up with them in the clouds and meet the Lord in the air."*

He said that I had so badly mistimed my tackle that the poor Baptist player was launched into the air and that was why he called it a Rapture tackle as the experience described by Paul in his first epistle to the Thessalonians is called the 'Rapture'. Cledan certainly had a great sense of humour.

It was during the second year that I was sent to see Archbishop Glyn Simon for possible expulsion from the College. It was my own fault as I was of the impression that we were being trained to present the Gospel to the unsaved as well as to Christians. However, there seemed to be limits to this perspective that I did not understand.

Whilst talking with some of the Ordinands one day, we discussed the matter as to how we might engage with people whom the Church and the socially respectable, possibly regarded as pariahs. In the days of Jesus, He touched the lepers (Matthew 8:1-5) and engaged with outcast Samaritans (John 4:1-42). We were struck by the comment in verse 9 that *"...Jews do not associate with Samaritans"*. We pondered as to what were the groups of today that the Church and the socially respectable might regard as 'Samaritans'.

One thing led to another and we decided that we would visit a striptease club in Cardiff. I hasten to add that we did not go with the intention of having a lewd night out but to seek opportunities of engaging with both the clientele and the striptease artists. We sat at different tables leaving spaces for other customers to join us. The evening went very well and we learned a lot. Well, I certainly did. We noted that the 'girls' would pick on a man at a table to assist her with her act. Unfortunately, one of our Ordinands was chosen to do this, and you could say that he took to it like a duck to water. What should have taken several minutes was completed with great alacrity in what must have been a record time. Apart from that one unfortunate incident, the evening was a success. I invited one of the 'girls' to have a drink with those at my table. She agreed.

We introduced ourselves as students training to be priests. To say that she was startled would be an underestimation. We explained that it was extremely unlikely that anyone at the club would be a 'church attending Christian' and that we felt the only way they would have an opportunity to engage with a Christian was for Christians to go to such establishments.

A wonderful conversation then unfolded in which she told us her story. She was amazingly open and poured out the things that had happened to her that eventually led her to becoming a Striptease Artist. Our hearts went out to her and when we said that Jesus died to rescue people like her and us, she replied that it may be true but that the Church would never accept her. I felt totally inadequate in attempting to respond to her. All that I could say was that she would be welcome in any church that I would eventually lead. At the end of the conversation, she thanked us for coming to the club and for taking the time to speak with her. Then she startled us by asking us if she could visit us at our 'place of work' as we had had the courage to visit her at her 'place of work'.

We all readily agreed and arrangements were made for me to pick her up the following day and bring her to the college.

When I arrived at her guest house, she had two of her friends with her and asked if they could come with her. I agreed, but there was just one small problem. I was driving a Triumph Spitfire sports car, one of the last vestiges of my previous life, and it was designed for two people only. Undeterred, her two friends got onto, not into, the car and squeezed their legs behind the two seats whilst sitting on top of the boot. It was a lovely summer's day. Can you imagine the scene? There was I, driving a small sports car with three gorgeous girls crammed into it. Each time I came to a traffic light, I prayed that the lights would be green, or should I say that I prayed that the bottom light would be on as I was colour blind. The prayers were not answered as every light that we came to had the top light on. As I waited for the bottom light to come on, the people in the cars around me stared and some of the occupants made unseemly remarks. The girls didn't seem to mind as they said that they were used to it.

As I approached the college, I breathed a huge sigh of relief. However, when I turned into the driveway there was a car wanting to come out. It was the car of the Principal of the college. Being a born gentleman, he reversed his car back to a turning point. I breathed another sigh of relief as I parked. But when we got out of the car, I turned around and there he was. It was the Principal. I remember him saying that he was glad that I had brought some friends to the college as the college was not a holy ghetto because it welcomed visitors. He asked to be introduced to the girls. I introduced the first young lady as June. Stretching out his hand towards her he said, "Hello June, and what line of business are you in?" When she replied that she was a Striptease Artist he nearly had apoplexy. He seemed to lose a considerable amount of bodily control. Quickly turning to the coloured girl next to her, I introduced him to Mary. This time, when he stretched out his hand to her, his mouth seemed to have lost a good deal of coordination. He said, "An Ur Wha Ur Wha Ur Wha Ur..." Mary was very gracious and put him out of his misery by saying, "I'm not a

29

Striptease Artist". On hearing this, he gathered a semblance of control, only to lose it altogether when she continued by saying, "I'm a Bunny Girl in the Playboy Club in London and Steve was with us in *Stripperama* last night."

I think she could have left the last part out, but in any case, the loss of bodily control in the Principal now reached to his knees. He seemed to do some strange kind of bending exercise as the colour visibly drained from him. It was more than he could take. Looking at his watch he muttered that he was going to be late and had to go quickly. I think if he had been introduced to the third girl he may have passed out. The third girl made the understatement of the year when she remarked that he seemed to have found that a little difficult.

We went to the college common room and there awaiting us were the Ordinands who were at the striptease club the night before together with a number of others. Each of the girls told their stories with confidence and they were greatly impressed by the response that they received. June asked what advice would they give her if she wanted to become a Christian. Although she was given a wide range of responses, she was still interested. On the way home, she asked me if I could put her in touch with a church in London that would accept her and not judge her. I didn't know any churches in London as I was a fairly new Christian myself, but I said that I would do my best and be in touch with her. Some while later I contacted her and gave her the name of Holy Trinity Brompton. They told me that they were doing a lot of work with the marginalised and that she would be most welcome. June went to the church and became a Christian. She said that her new life was wonderful and that she was successful in her application for employment at Harrods. The store was almost opposite Holy Trinity in Knightsbridge. She was still in touch with her two friends and had been encouraging them to follow her.

That evening, there appeared a notice on the college notice board. It stated that in future all invitations for guests to visit the college had to have prior permission from the Principal. In my mail pigeon hole alongside the notice board was an invitation for

Steve Morgan to meet with the Principal immediately after the evening meal. It proved to be a difficult meeting and he told me he would be making a request to the Archbishop for me to meet with him to determine whether or not I should be allowed to continue as an Ordinand.

When I met with the Archbishop, he had received a full report from the Principal. The Archbishop took me aback when he asked if there was anything that I wanted to say before he confirmed my expulsion. Then came one of those moments when words flowed without any prior preparation. I found myself asking if I could put some questions to him. He agreed. The first question that I asked was, "Are you the Archbishop of Wales?" He looked somewhat bemused and said, "Of course I am. What a silly question." My second question was, "Then, as Archbishop of Wales, are you responsible for all the Anglican churches and congregations in Wales or are you responsible for the whole of Wales?" He replied, "The whole of Wales". My third question was, "If you are responsible for the whole of Wales, does that mean that you are responsible for all the prisons, brothels, drug dens and clip joints etc?" He replied, "Yes". I then found myself asking him if I could tell him a story.

I didn't know what I was going to say but the words just flowed. I asked him to imagine a trainee AA Patrolman driving to the AA Training College when he came across a distressed lady standing alongside her car. The trainee stops to enquire as to what is the problem. She says that her car has broken down and that she is frightened and was unable to contact anyone. He proceeds to repair her car, and with great gratitude she then was able to continue her journey. The trainee then makes his way to the college. A little while later the incident comes to the attention of the college authorities and they expel him for repairing her car prior to becoming qualified as an AA Patrolman. I then asked the Archbishop what he thought of the story. He said that it was ridiculous that the trainee should be expelled, to which I replied, "That is exactly what you are about to do to me". He protested that I should not speak to him like that, but I said that I acknowledged him as being a true man of God, and he surely was, and that I was confident that he knew that I was right. I told him that if he expelled me, I would not hold it against him and I would be confident that the Lord would lead me to another context in which I could minister to the saved and the marginalised. I asked him that if he expelled me would he go to Stripperama and tell the people working there the difference that Jesus had made to his life. He replied that he would not be seen dead in such a place. I responded by saying that I could only respect that viewpoint if he was prepared to send someone in his place and with his permission to take the Good News of the Gospel to the unsaved and marginalised who were there. A wry smile came across his face and he leant forward and shook my hand telling me that I was to go back into college and continue as an Ordinand.

The college accommodated other students from the university as well as Ordinands. When it came to preparations for the infamous University Rag Week, one of the dental students with us upbraided us for never taking part. He said that we were too aloof and sober minded to engage in such an activity and that set us apart from other students.

I felt that he was goading us and to me that was like a red rag to a bull. I was determined to set up a Rag Week stunt that had never been done before so as to lay the bogey once and for all. Going through the annuls of Rag Week, I found that one of the stunts that had never been accomplished was to take Castle Coch, a small castle and tourist attraction on the outskirts of Cardiff, and hold it to ransom. So that was it. It was Castle Coch or bust. Considerable time was spent hatching the plot and we needed help from other university students to make it happen. By the time it came for the taking of Castle Coch we had gathered over fifty students.

The first part of the plan was for a small party of twelve students to visit the castle pretending to be from the university Archeological Department. We carried 'equipment' for the task in rucksacks and made our way to the castle. On arriving we told the Curator that we were from the university Archeological

Department and that we had been commissioned to do a survey of the area. He was very obliging and let us all in. Twelve went in but only ten came out. We left two secreted away in the castle together with the equipment that would be needed to carefully take off the entrance door without doing any damage.

Meanwhile, the remaining students who had volunteered to be a part of the stunt gathered at the bottom of the road leading to the castle. At the appointed time the entrance door to the castle was taken off and in we all went. It was a bitterly cold night and so we decided to leave a 'skeleton staff' on duty whilst the remainder of us went to the pub at the bottom of the road leading to the castle. All was going very smoothly and we were enjoying our libations when a cacophony of noise was heard approaching the pub. Looking out of the pub window, we saw a rich variety of police vehicles speeding toward the castle. Police motorbikes, vans, and cars sped past the pub. The gathered noise of all these vehicles with sirens blasting had the same effect on the clientele of the pub goers as the starting gun at the *Le Mans 24 Hour Road Race.*

Many of our group rushed out of the pub and drove off from the car park at a rate of knots, leaving just a handful of students behind. Apparently, some of the students had borrowed several roadside lamps from road workings nearby the castle and used them to have a look around the castle. Local residents had seen lights moving around in the castle and telephoned the police. I felt terrible. It had all gone wrong and I was responsible. What could I do? At the very least I felt that I had to go to the castle and to see what was happening. One of the Dental students volunteered to go with me together with two of the female Domestic Science students from the college in Llandaff. They pretended to be our girlfriends and we walked toward the police cordon holding hands appropriately.

We asked the police what was happening but they wouldn't tell us. We explained that we were four friends out for our nightly walk and asked if we could just go to the next bend in the road before returning. They let us through, but at the bend we separated. The two female students doubled back to an awaiting car to take them back to their halls of residence in Llandaff. Meanwhile, the two of us made our way to the castle. We heard the sound of police officers shouting at students to stop so that they could be arrested. Lights were flashing through the woods to spot individuals who decided to decline the invitation for arrest. It wasn't safe to stay on the road so we crawled on our stomachs, inching our way towards the castle, stopping now and then as the police lights that were searching for students came close to us. It only seemed a matter of minutes before the noise died down and the police vehicles left, transporting their cargo of students.

When we got to the road leading to the castle, we noticed there were only two police officers left who were patrolling up and down the road. When we felt it was safe, we tiptoed across the road and went into the dry moat and, crawling anti-clockwise so as not to be seen, we made our way to the drawbridge. Voices were heard coming towards us, so we crawled under the drawbridge near the point where it met the ground. A police officer and the Curator came and stood directly above us. Their conversation was most revealing. No damage had been done to the castle and so the Police were going to threaten the arrested students with 'Breaking and Entering' and 'Theft'. The officer explained to the Curator why the threatened charges were just that, threats, and why these charges would not be able to stand in a court of law anyway. He went on to say that his intention was to frighten the students so as to deter them from any further such stunts in the future.

After they left, we made our way back to our car. I just had to find out where they had taken the students, so we drove to the nearby Taffs Well Police Station. I said to the Sergeant at the Police Station that I was worried for the safety of a group of student friends of mine as they had been on a Rag Week stunt in the area and I had not heard from them. It was now past midnight. He made a telephone call to the main Police Station at Pontypridd and confirmed that the students were there. Overhearing the telephone conversation, I heard the Sergeant ask what he should do. When he repeated that answer of keeping me there till someone came to pick me up, I hastily departed the station and swiftly drove away from the scene.

When I got to the Pontypridd Police Station, the Sergeant at the desk invited me to follow him. When I asked where we were going he said it was to the cells. I protested and asked on what charge was I being taken to the cells. He said that the charges were 'Breaking and Entering' and 'Theft'. Remembering what the police officer had said to the Curator at the castle, I replied that the charges could not be made because the two students that had been left in the castle broke out not in, and that the roadside lamps had only been transferred from public property, the road, to further public property, the castle. His reply was, "Who do you think you are, some … Philadelphia lawyer?" I was then invited to vacate the premises forthwith. Returning to the car, my friend and I were pondering whether we should return home or wait for a while to see if the students would be released. However, it was only a matter of minutes later that we saw all the students leaving the Police Station. It proved to be a very long night as we shuttled all the students back to their halls of residence.

I got to bed after 6am, absolutely shattered, and missed the morning service for prayers in the college chapel. I arrived at breakfast more than a little bleary eyed and was just starting to enjoy a full cooked breakfast when the college telephone rang. It was a call from the Archbishop to the Principal of the college. When the Principal returned his face was ashen. Resuming his place at the breakfast table, he stood, braced himself and announced that the telephone call was from the Archbishop. The Archbishop told the Principal that he was having his breakfast, and as was his usual custom, he began to read his *Western Mail*. His eyes alighted upon an article on the front page which was entitled *"Twenty Students Arrested At Surrender Of Castle Coch"*. Underneath the article there was a reference to a picture on page four. Turning to page four, the Archbishop was horrified to see one of the Principal's Ordinands being a perfect gentleman and allowing a young lady to enter a police van before him. The Principal was then asked by the Archbishop as to what kind of establishment he was running. There were certain tell tale signs that the Principal was embarrassed and rattled by his conversation with the Archbishop. He was now red in the face and gathering momentum for an outburst. He had two distinctive mannerisms which now became somewhat exaggerated. He sucked air in through his teeth and his right hand extended, palm uppermost, with his thumb and forefinger pressing against each other.

When the air came out he said, "Payne (the Ordinand in the photograph) and Morgan, follow me". I tried vainly to put on as innocent a looking face as I could whilst pointing to my chest and saying, "Me?" He insisted that I must have been involved as my burgeoning reputation for such frolics went before me. We sat down in his study and were given a really good dressing down. The Principal finished by asking me to choose between Ordination or, in his words, "continuing such Gestapo activities until you are thrown out once and for all".

All went well for a while, until the Principal got to hear that I was often out very late at night and didn't get back to the college until the early hours. I would take a flask of soup and some bread and go to Sophia Gardens or Cardiff Docks looking for the homeless. I learnt so much from them and spent many hours just hearing their stories and on a few occasions was able to pray for them. Most of them really appreciated the fact that someone cared for them, whilst sharing the bread and soup, and spending time with them.

There were numerous heartbreaking stories and I came to realise that these people, who were cast as some of the modern day lepers of society, had physical and spiritual needs that cried out for understanding and mercy. It amazed me that most of them had never taken drugs or alcohol before they became homeless. Some were abused by parents or other relatives; some were heartbroken when spouses left them; some lost jobs and couldn't pay their rent or mortgages any more. A soldier told me he lost his leg whilst fighting for his country and he just could not cope with the fact that he had killed a human being, a so called 'enemy soldier'. He had recurring nightmares and soiled his bed most nights. This brought him humiliation and anger and eventually his family abandoned him.

On another occasion, I met a young woman who had run away from her pimp. When she saw me, she was terrified. I explained that I was a Christian and had soup and bread for her and wondered if I could do anything to help her. We sat in the corner of a derelict building and she poured out her heart to me. Her parents had apparently used her for prostitution since she was only six years old. The income that they had enabled them to pay their rent and buy all the alcohol and drugs they ever needed.

She was now twenty three years old but she looked much older. She had run away from her pimp because her last 'client' had beaten her so badly. She allowed me to tell her about the love that Jesus had for her and that He believed that she was worth dying for. I prayed a prayer that Jesus would rescue her from her situation and, as I was about to leave, she stood up and began to unbutton her dress. The only way that she could express her gratitude was to offer her body. I put my arms around her and we wept together. I cried out another prayer that Jesus would rescue her. Before we parted we made an arrangement to meet the following night as I would contact every agency I could think of that could help her in her plight. That was the night that the Principal caught me as I climbed out of a window to meet with her.

I told him the story of the young woman and his heart absolutely melted. He gave me the privilege of seeing a side to him that I did not know existed. He gave me his blessing and asked me to let him know the outcome the following morning. I was devastated when the young woman failed to turn up. The Principal asked me the following morning before breakfast how I got on the previous night. When I told him that she did not show up, he put his hand on my shoulder, looked in my eyes, and then quickly turned and walked off. The poise and dignity of the man would not allow me to see the emotion that he was surely feeling and I respected him greatly for that.

My last year in college was in 1971 and during that year I married my first wife, Marilyn. My cousin Susan had arranged a blind date for me with one of her friends in work. Marilyn was a manager in the Post Office Headquarters in Cardiff. I had always been quite gauche with members of the opposite sex, but Marilyn was so easy to talk to that conversation just flowed. Towards the end of the blind date, we found ourselves close to a beach just off the Lavernock Road, near Penarth. My cousin and her boyfriend, now husband, Richard were in the car whilst Marilyn and I walked outside. When we got back to the car, the car windows were completely steamed up. We laughed quietly at the sight and just carried on talking and getting to know each other until they came out for air. We fell in love very quickly and were married within months.

4

From Llanharan to the Cathedral

After studying at St Michael's College for four years, I was Ordained at Llandaff Cathedral. It was a glorious experience that very soon dissipated as the problem of where Marilyn and I were going to live began to emerge. At the time, we were living above a hairdresser's in Llandaff High Street. I commuted every day to serve my curacy in the parish of Llanharan as the parish did not have a house for a curate. Despite assurances that the parish would be buying a house for us to live in, there seemed to be delay after delay. The landlady of our flat in Llandaff wanted to know when we would be leaving so that she could advertise for a new tenant. We finally gave her a date in spite of the fact we had nowhere to go. We were due to vacate the flat on a Saturday, and yet on the Monday before we still had nowhere to go.

I contacted the Bishop of Llandaff, Eryl Thomas, and explained our plight. He quickly got back to me and told me to arrange to meet with the Dean of the Cathedral, the Venerable J F Williams, as there was a house vacant in the parish following the departure of the curate. The Bishop said the Dean had agreed that moving into the curate's house would give us some breathing space to finally sort out our accommodation at Llanharan.

A meeting was hastily arranged and the Dean and I met in his study. I was anxious to pick up the key so that we could clean the house in readiness for our move. However, the Dean just kept on talking and asking me questions about my life story. Then, after over an hour, he at last handed me the key whilst saying I had got the job. I was taken aback. I had only come for the key to the house, but the Dean said he had conducted an interview for the position of curate at the Cathedral! I protested that I had only recently started as the curate of Llanharan. He said he would sort it all out and that he wanted me to be his curate. Numbed by this offer, I returned to our flat and told Marilyn I had not only been given the key to the curate's house, but that I had been offered the position of curate in the Cathedral as well. We were as elated as we were nervous at the prospect.

It wasn't long after meeting the Dean that I finished my curacy at Llanharan and joined the staff at the Cathedral as the Assistant Curate. We lived in a lovely house near the Cathedral and the congregation made me feel very much at home. It was here that my wife Marilyn gave birth to our first child Sarah. She had always wanted to be a full time mother and offered her resignation as a Manager for the Post Office. I have to say that without her salary coming in we found it increasingly hard to make ends meet. It got to the stage where we received in the post the red final demand for the electricity bill, but all we had left was our Offertory envelope for the next Sunday's collection. We were at that time tithing our income and set aside ten percent of my salary each month. As soon as it came in, we put our tithe into the collection envelope. But this month was different. Despite Marilyn being an excellent housekeeper and extremely frugal with money, we had come to the point where we could no longer manage. The question then arose – do we use the money in our collection envelope or do we trust God? We spoke about it and prayed at great length. In the end we decided we would make an act of faith and put our tithe into the Cathedral collection. We also agreed I should take the electricity bill and place it under the white cloth on the main altar. As I did so, I told the Lord that this was an act of faith in believing He would always provide for us. He is after all *'Jehovah Jirah'*, which means 'God provides'.

This act of faith was an act in which I was challenged to practice what I had recently been preaching at the Cathedral about the tension between faith and feelings. If, in our Christian walk, our actions are primarily determined by what we feel, then our faith will almost always lag behind and be significantly unfulfilled. If, however, our actions are primarily determined by our faith, then our feelings will have the opportunity of catching up with that faith and we will experience a greater measure of spiritual growth and maturity. I have to say on my way back to our house that day I was feeling a real mixture of faith and fear. I had made an act of faith on our behalf but was honestly still fearful of the consequences.

That night, as Marilyn and I prayed together, we had a marvellous sense of peace about it all. It seemed as if our emotions had indeed caught up with our faith even though we were still in a financial crisis. The post normally arrived early and as we sat down for breakfast we opened our mail. On this particular day I had a letter from the Bishop. As I opened it, I gasped. In with the letter was a cheque for the exact amount, to the very penny, of our electricity bill. Apparently, the Bishop had received a sum of money from a benefactor which he was asked to distribute between all the curates in the diocese according to the number of children that they had. How amazing! We were awestruck and became very emotional as the build-up of the pressure from our situation just came flooding out.

After we composed ourselves, we contacted the Bishop and told him our story. He thanked us for getting back to him so soon and said he was blessed to have been the agent of our rescue. It is true that some of the most powerful lessons we can learn in the Christian life are those learnt when we are taken to the very brink. Just when all seems lost and there is no rescue in sight, the Lord intervenes and shows how much He loves us and desires to provide for us.

A short while after this I received a small inheritance and we were able to buy our first brand new car – a Morris Marina. This proved an excellent investment for the somniferous effect it had on Sarah when she could not sleep at night. Within a mile of setting off, Sarah would be fast asleep. Then we would return home and carefully carry her from the car, leaving all the car doors open, walk through the front door, leaving the front door open and placing her in her cot. Then we would retrace our steps and close all the doors as quietly as we could. We didn't care how daft this looked to our neighbours, it was a case of needs must. Indeed, years later, when we were able to go on a camping holidays in France, Sarah and her sister Emma would be asleep almost the entire journey.

I got on very well with Bishop Eryl Thomas and we enjoyed his company and that of his wife Jean. However, when it came to Cathedral services we had a real mixture of hilarious incidents and temper tantrums. On one occasion, I made the fatal mistake of arranging a Diocesan Youth Event at the Cathedral in which all the deaneries of the Diocese took it in turns to make a contribution. The mistake was to do with the date. It turned out to be the day that Wales were playing Australia in Cardiff.

One of the Cathedral parishioners was a member of the Welsh Rugby Union Committee and he always gave the Bishop a ticket for the home internationals. Not to be outdone, the Bishop gave me a set of strict instructions concerning a plan he had so as to mitigate somewhat his absence from the game. Before the event, I was to have a rehearsal in the morning in which all the deanery contributions had to be timed. Then, when the event took place in the afternoon, I had to announce all the contributions and slowly move out of sight, go to the back door of the Cathedral and then run like a scalded rabbit up the hill at the side of the Cathedral with a key to the verger's house firmly clenched in my fist. The verger was instructed to leave his television on for my arrivals. Yes, arrivals. I was to run up the hill, get the latest score from the television, run back down the hill, and then walk in a dignified fashion behind the Bishop's throne and whisper the score and scorers to the Bishop. There he was in all his finery with staff in hand, mitre on head and wearing a splendid cope, looking exceptionally dignified and poised.

It was the day when Wales won 24-0. I would creep behind his throne and whisper, "Bennett scored a penalty", to which the Bishop replied in his best ventriloquist's voice, "Great". Phil

Bennett, the Wales outside half scored four penalties that day. The news of the penalties didn't seem to move the Bishop that much, but the first time I told him that Wales had scored a try his emotions got the better of him and he gave a little shout, "Marvellous!" Then I heard a response from the clergyman sitting in front of the Bishop, "Yes my Lord, I think this one is very good", referring to the latest deanery contribution. I just don't know what comes over me at times like this because I simply lose all sense of decorum. I said to the Bishop, "Unless you can control yourself better I'm not going to tell you any more scores." The Bishop replied, "Morgan, how much to you value your life?"

The next time I came to give him the score I said, "Hold on to your seat, Wales have scored another try". He sat there, motionless, and didn't say a word. All went according to plan except that towards the end of the event, I was absolutely shattered with all the running up and down the hill. By the time it came to announcing the last item I was very much out of breath and had to pause to take in gulps of air between every other word. At the end of the service the Bishop came up to me and said, "Morgan, let that be a lesson to you. Never arrange anything for me again without first consulting the Wales Rugby calendar". We laughed together and I asked him how he managed to control himself when the clergyman in front of him responded to his exclamation of "Marvellous?" He gave no reply but the glint in his eye was enough.

It only took another month before I got into trouble again. In December, there was a Christmas service in the Cathedral that was to be televised. The person who was in charge of all the arrangements for the ceremonials in the Cathedral had taught me that the golden rule for a rookie like myself was to walk in straight lines, always make a ninety degree turn and place the palms of the hands together with fingers pointing slightly upwards. If ever I got lost and didn't know where I should be or what I should do, then to keep on walking until someone grabbed me or told me what I should be doing. This might sound hilarious, but it certainly kept me fit as I must have walked miles around the Cathedral during my time there. At any rate, the BBC were televising live a Christmas service.

The Bishop and clergy were gathered in the St David's Chapel before the service and I was the Bishop's Chaplain. Moments before the service was due to begin I was called away to attend to a matter that would normally have taken only a minute to deal with. However, it took longer as I had to negotiate the television cameras and an elderly couple who asked me if I could find them a seat. Although I directed them to one of the stewards on duty, I was late getting back to the Chapel.

The Bishop was furious with me and said, "Morgan, give me my hat and stick or take the ... service yourself." I wanted the ground to swallow me up as I looked at the stern and affronted faces of the clergy. My heart was pounding but my brain was functioning quite well, and I was pleased I was able to remember where I should be and what I should be doing – right up until the time came for the Bishop to pronounce the blessing at the end of the service. Then my mind went blank and I froze.

I was standing with my back to the camera that was ready to zoom in on the Bishop. The Bishop motioned with his head and I thought he wanted me to come closer to him so I slowly inched my way towards him, not knowing that I was still obscuring the line of sight of the camera. The Bishop parted his lips and in his best ventriloquist's voice said, "Organ, get out o' the hay." I then looked around and saw the camera behind me. I staggered backwards and was now shoulder to shoulder with the Bishop. He took a firm grasp of my right hand and promptly prayed the Blessing.

When we had all processed back to the St David's Chapel at the end of the service and the blessing had been prayed for those in the procession, the clergy dispersed in all directions with unseemly haste rather than hear the Episcopal verbal eruption that ensued. When I got home, the first thing my wife said to me was that she had watched the programme and it finished very nicely with a close up of the Bishop and me. I told her that 'close up' nearly cost me my job and I could still feel the butterflies in my stomach from the telling off I had received. Marilyn was very supportive and understanding – I just stood there as she convulsed with laughter with tears streaming down her face. It was one of those infectious laughs and I soon joined her.

A few weeks later I met with the Bishop and he asked me what I was doing for Christmas that year. I said that I didn't know as it was too far in the future. He said that one thing was for sure – I would not be his Chaplain again for a televised service, and we both laughed together. He said reassuringly that his bark was worse than his bite. Nevertheless, he frightened the living daylights out of one of the Minor Canons one morning who had arrived late and 'Matins' was already being said. As he approached the choir stalls he genuflected. Big mistake. The Bishop exploded afterwards, "To arrive late for Matins is a sin, but to arrive and genuflect with your pyjama leg showing from under your cassock is a sin against the Holy Ghost!" The Bishop had a wonderful way with words. This incident and a number of others were sources of great amusement that we shared with each other whenever we went to visit him and his wife after his retirement.

In spite of being very happily married to my wife Marilyn, I would experience waves of emotions that left me bewildered and confused. There were times when I felt worthless, unloved, unwanted, and rejected. These feelings were not being generated from tensions in family or any other source that I could identify. They were within me and I did not have a clue why they were molesting me with such violence. Waves of dread would sweep over me and many times, after the morning services had been completed, I would go home, take a shower, and have a complete change of clothes because they were saturated with perspiration. I knew that I needed help, but because I didn't have any understanding as to why this was happening, I shied off from speaking to anyone.

Eventually it got so bad that, with Marilyn's encouragement, I made an appointment to speak to Canon Norman Autton, who was the senior chaplain at the Heath Hospital in Cardiff. I didn't have the courage to tell him the real reason why I wanted to see him and so the appointment was made to talk concerning the Healing Ministry. When I met with him, he gave me a great deal of advice and commended me to read a number of books. Feeling comfortable in his presence, I opened up about what was happening to me at a personal level. He listened attentively with obvious care and concern, and he said that I needed 'Inner Healing'. I did not know what this meant as I had never heard of it before. He gave me a brief overview of what 'Inner Healing' meant and commended me to sign up for a conference on the subject at an Anglican church in Hounslow. I was so grateful to him for his time and wisdom. When I returned home, I immediately signed up for the next Inner Healing conference that was being held.

At the conference, I learnt so much about human brokenness and how to pray and minister in a variety of contexts. This was a banquet for my spirit but, as much as I was captivated by such insight and revelation, I was also sinking into despair and loneliness once again. I was confused by such an array of emotions and felt quite disorientated. Then it was announced that there would be a public service of prayer for healing on the Thursday evening which was open to the public, conference members and parishioners. As the service progressed, I became very emotional and prayed to the Lord that I felt I could not go on any longer. He just had to do something.

When the invitation was given to people for them to come forward for prayer, I got to my feet very slowly and with tear filled eyes walked to the first couple in the Ministry Team that were free. They were husband and wife and they asked me what it was that they could pray about. When I had finished speaking out all the negative emotions that were overwhelming me, they asked if I had any idea as to where such emotions were coming from. I said that I didn't have the first clue. The husband then startled me by saying that it didn't matter at all that I had no idea as to where these emotions were coming from because they would simply ask the Holy Spirit to give them the revelation that was needed. His wife agreed with him in a manner that was calm and caring, but above all totally convincing.

I had never encountered such faith and assurance. They prayed to the Holy Spirit and asked Him to grant them the knowledge as to what was the root of the problem. Moments later, the husband said that he felt that the Holy Spirit had shown him that when my mother was three months pregnant with me, my father left her for another woman. During that time my mother was overwhelmed with emotions of anger, grief, worthlessness, rejection, and fear. His wife then explained that these very emotions my mother was experiencing were also being felt by me in the womb and became a part of my post-natal life. Then the husband said that although my father returned to my mother three months later, the damage had been done and that no amount of post-natal love and care could undo what had been done to me whilst in the womb. I knew in my spirit that what had been said was true and this indeed was the root of my problems. The couple prayed for me but also explained that in order to receive the fullest measure of healing I would need to find the right place and person. I asked them to elaborate and they explained there were Christian Homes of Healing that could help, but it would require a considerable time commitment so be set aside for this. I was so struck by what I had heard that it was not until hours later that I wished I had asked the husband how on earth could he have known my father had indeed returned three months after he left my mother.

When I returned home, I asked my mother about these things and she confirmed that it was exactly as the Holy Spirit had revealed. It was a difficult conversation as I tried to explain to her that she was not to blame for what had been done to me in the womb. It saddened me to see the distress that this revelation caused her, but the fact of speaking it out did bring us closer together and eventually this led to her seeking the Ministry of Healing at the Divine Healing Mission in Crowhurst.

I went to Crowhurst myself in the hope that this would be the context in which I might receive the Inner Healing I needed.

However, it was such a long way away that I decided against it. It was explained to me that I would have needed to stay there for a short period of time and that it could take several visits. I didn't feel that I could justify taking my annual holiday time away from my young family. Perhaps this was the excuse that I needed to step back from making the time commitment. Then again, perhaps it was a matter of pride and embarrassment that prevented me from telling the Dean that I needed time off for this ministry. My prayer was that the Lord would find the time and space for me to receive this ministry one day.

In spite of my unresolved issues, I continued to preach what I believed to be true concerning the ministry of healing. Jesus still heals today. The Gospel readings set out in the Anglican Prayer Book were full of wonderful accounts of Jesus healing people and also commissioning His disciples to preach the Gospel and heal the sick.

The Dean of the Cathedral, the Venerable J.F. Williams was a very pastoral priest and easy to engage with. However, he was having difficulty in handling the complaints that were coming his way as a result of my preaching. Eventually, he asked me to write out my sermons in full and submit them to him for editing. This proved very difficult. So I resolved that if he was going to edit my sermons then I would go into as much detail as possible in the knowledge he would have to read more about the Ministry of Healing than I would have dared to preach.

It wasn't very long before he realised what I was doing and called me into his study at the Deanery. We had a wonderful conversation in which he admitted that he had great personal difficulty believing in the validity of the Church's Ministry of Healing today but acknowledged it was a passion in my life that I simply could not let go. He asked me to tone down my sermons if he relinquished his editorial demands. We agreed. I had the consolation of knowing that I had gained his respect and he would now trust me to be a little more circumspect. Circumspection, or wisdom, dictated that I preached the same messages but that I would choose to use language that would encourage enquiry rather than confront disbelief.

My relationship with the Dean was one of great personal respect and this was well illustrated by an incident at a mid-week Eucharist service. A lovely lady by the name of Clarabella Thompson had brought her young grandson to the service. It was the first time that he had attended the Cathedral and he was instructed not to make a noise and to be quiet. You could hear a pin drop before the service began as the congregation were either sitting or praying in reverent silence. Then, in walked the Dean and his Server. It wasn't very long into the service when the little boy turned to his grandmother and enquiringly said, "Nan?". Clarabella quickly whispered to him to be quiet. Moments later he again turned to his grandmother and said, "But Nan." Again she told him to be quiet. By this time Clarabella was getting agitated as a few heads turned towards them both. However, her grandchild was not to be put off and this time he spoke in a loud voice and said, "Nan." Clarabella then said in a loud whisper, "What is it?" to which the little boy, speaking out loud said, "Nan, you told me to be quiet, but that man up there hasn't stopped talking since the time he came in." He then pointed to the Dean. The congregation was divided by a dual response. Some gasped in horror whilst others tried to hide their amusement.

The Dean stopped the service, came out from behind the altar, and standing at the altar rail he addressed the congregation, and then the little boy. He reminded the congregation of the phrase *'suffer the little children to come unto me'*. He went on to tell the congregation that the word 'suffer' did not mean 'to put up with', it meant 'to welcome'. He then asked the little boy's name and went on to ask him if he would like him to tell the little boy what it was that he was doing and what it was that he was talking about. The little boy said, "Yes please" and in a few sentences the Dean beautifully explained in language that the child could easily understand what was happening.

The Dean had managed to turn a very embarrassing situation into one in which he took the interruption and made it into a positive and affirming moment in the service. Afterwards, as was his custom, the Dean stood at the door to meet everyone. Clarabella began to apologise to the Dean, but he stopped her and said he was not embarrassed and in fact it had given him the opportunity to explain to the entire congregation in the simplest of terms what was the role of a priest and the meaning of the Eucharist. Then he whispered loudly to her that he felt the congregation needed to hear what he had said. With an affirming smile he ruffled the boy's hair and said, "Well done." This was the Dean at his consummate best. He was, at heart, a true pastor.

Several years later, the Dean and I both attended an Induction service and in the vestry, the Dean, who had retired by this time, asked all present to be silent as he had something to say. He made a public apology to me and said that he was wrong in rejecting the Ministry of Healing as he was now convinced that the Ministry of Healing was for today. There was a stunned silence after he had finished speaking. He spoke to me afterwards and related how an experience of Jesus healing someone whom he knew had changed his mind. He thanked me for my preaching and said that although he rejected it at the time, it nevertheless formed a part of his personal spiritual journey. I had always had a great affection for 'JF' but my admiration of him soared in that vestry experience.

Whilst at the Cathedral, there were two ministry situations in which I learned a great deal about the Ministry of Healing, and both of them were with regards to people who were suffering from multiple sclerosis. In the first situation, there was an opportunity of praying for a lady who was a parishioner of the Cathedral. She had been ill for several years and was in an advanced stage of multiple sclerosis. Over a period of many months I brought to her home the sacrament of Holy Communion and she received prayers for healing. Then, one day, as she was being prayed for, her countenance seemed to glisten. A time of silence followed during which her face shone and a wonderful smile radiated a look of awe and wonder. When she opened her eyes, she said she felt that she had been in the Lord's presence and wanted to go back. I told her that I thought it would be appropriate for me to leave and speak with her later that day. A few hours later she telephoned me and asked me to come back as she had had a remarkable experience and did not know what it meant. On arriving at her house, she couldn't wait to tell me that when I left earlier, she decided to go to bed with the intention of lying down and praying that the Lord would continue to bless her with His presence. When she got to the bedroom she suddenly felt a remarkable strengthening in her body. So she laid her walking sticks against the wall, and with complete muscular coordination she walked to the bed. Then she laid on the bed with eyes closed and felt her legs doing bicycle movements. She was bathing in the Lord's presence. All she could pray was, "Thank you", over and over again.

After a while, she opened her eyes to see her legs doing the bicycle movements. To her astonishment, her legs were not moving, but the experience of feeling as if they were doing bicycle movements continued for several minutes. Then, of course, she asked me what this experience meant. I confessed I didn't have the first clue, but suggested we should pray together and ask the Holy Spirit to reveal the meaning to us of this strange experience. I found myself saying to her that she had been given an experience of her perfectly restored resurrection body. This puzzled both of us and neither of us felt we had received any further revelation. Why was she granted this experience?

It wasn't until several years later that a partial answer to the question occurred. During the intervening time, I had moved from the Cathedral to the parish of Neath and from there to the Rectorial Benefice of Merthyr Tydfil and Cyfarthfa. One day I received a telephone call to let me know that the lady was at the Heath Hospital in Cardiff and was a terminal cancer patient. So, with a heavy heart, I went to see her. In praying for her beforehand, I repented of being annoyed with Him that this lovely Christian lady who had suffered so much with multiple sclerosis was now diagnosed with terminal cancer.

As I stood at her bedside, I was still wallowing in sorrow, anger and confusion. Feeling completely inadequate, I asked the absolutely banal question, "How are you feeling?" I was stunned at her response. She said that she had never felt better in all her life. I pulled up a chair and sitting at the bedside I asked her to tell me her story since we last met years ago.

Apparently, her condition deteriorated as expected by her doctors, and out of the blue she suddenly took a dramatic turn for the worse. Tests revealed that she had what the doctors described as incurable cancer. She recounted that the earlier experience of being in the presence of the Lord had increased her faith remarkably. There was no sense that He had let her down by not healing her. Instead, she decided that she wanted to have a significant part in her own funeral service by composing prayers. At this time, her condition was such that she was unable to write so she asked her two daughters to be present, and together with her husband, she dictated the prayers that she wanted prayed at her funeral service.

To her astonishment, the impact that this had on her husband and children resulted in them making a profession of faith. She said that she had prayed for a very long time that the people whom she loved the most, her husband and children, would become Christians, as the thought of being in heaven without them was breaking her heart. Now, in the knowledge that they had all committed their lives to Christ, she was contented to the depths of her soul. She said that if the only way for her loved ones to become Christians was for her to suffer with the diseases that her body was carrying, then it was all worthwhile. She had thanked the Lord for the privilege of suffering as the route to the answer of her greatest prayer petition – that her loved ones would become Christians and would one day meet with her again in heaven.

I appreciate that this story leaves us with a number of questions concerning God and His promise of healing, and the blessings that can come from human suffering and unanswered prayer. These are subjects that I will deal with in some detail in a further book called *A Training Manual for the Church's Ministry of Healing* that I am currently writing.

In the second story of another person with multiple sclerosis, the outcome was very different. The lady concerned was confined to bed and unable to attend to her everyday needs. Although I had been praying for her for many months, her condition had continued to deteriorate. Having recently returned from a Ministry of Healing conference in Holy Trinity, Hounslow, I asked her if I could pray a very different kind of prayer with her. I explained there are situations when prayer for healing seems to have no effect because there may be an underlying and unresolved hurt, wound or sin. In such a scenario, it is possible to pray for the Holy Spirit to bring into the person's conscious mind exactly what needs to be resolved. At this time, I had a close and trusting relationship with the lady and felt comfortable in asking her if she would be willing to receive such prayer. She agreed and I asked the Holy Spirit to reveal to her if there was any unresolved issue in her life that was preventing healing. Very quickly, she began to cry. Afterwards, she said that she wanted to tell me something of her story.

A number of years ago, she was involved in a car accident when she was pregnant. She had been badly injured and as a consequence was in a coma. During the time she was in the coma, her husband was told he had to make a choice. The mother and child could not both survive. He chose the option of the baby being aborted. Some while later, she came out of the coma and the first question that she asked was that of the welfare of her baby. The hospital staff delayed as much as they could before telling her that her baby had to be aborted in order to save her life. The instant she heard this, she said she felt that she had been a party to a murder. However, she did not tell anyone this, but kept it in her heart. Years later, she became ill and was eventually diagnosed with multiple sclerosis. On hearing the diagnosis, she prayed in her heart a prayer of thanks for the illness as this was, to her mind, a just punishment from God for being a party to the murder of her unborn baby. My immediate reaction was to want to tell her that she was wrong and that God would not do such a thing, but I felt a constraint in my spirit from saying this. Instead, I asked her to join with me in a time of prayer for the healing of this memory. During the time of prayer, she asked the Lord to forgive her husband for making the decision to abort her baby. She asked the

Lord to forgive the surgeon who performed the abortion, the medical staff who supported the surgeon, the driver of the car who was responsible for the accident, and finally, she forgave herself for embracing the perception that God had given her this disease as a punishment. After these prayers, she felt as if a great weight had been lifted from her and in the following weeks and months to the consternation of her doctors she regained strength in her body. When the day came that they told her she was in remission from multiple sclerosis she was over the moon as you can imagine. All bodily strength and functions were restored.

Dr S.I.McMillen wrote in his book *None of these Diseases*[1],

> Peace does not come in capsules! This is regrettable because medical science recognises that emotions such as fear, sorrow, envy, resentment and hatred are responsible for the majority of our sicknesses. Estimates vary from 60 per cent to nearly 100 per cent. Emotional stress can cause high blood pressure toxic loiter, migraine headaches, arthritis, apoplexy, heart trouble, gastrointestinal ulcers, and other diseases too numerous to mention. As physicians, we can prescribe medicine for the symptoms of these diseases, but we cannot do much for the underlying cause – emotional turmoil. *It is lamentable that peace does not come in capsules.*

In the story detailed above we have an illustration of how the body can react when trauma and the emotions generated remain unresolved. The story also illustrates that prayer for the healing of memories can have a profound effect on the physical body.

---

[1] S.I.Mcmillen MD 'None of These Diseases'. Lakeland 1980 p7

5

Under 'Neath' are the Everlasting Arms

In 1974, after my short time in the Cathedral, my family and I moved to Neath where I had responsibility for St Catherine's Church in the Melin area. Whilst at Neath, there were three experiences of healing that had a profound impact on me.

At one of our Holy Week services, I noticed two ladies sitting on their own, one was wearing dark glasses and holding a white stick. When it came time to receive the Sacrament, the blind lady was assisted by her companion to kneel down at the altar rail. When I came to minister to the blind lady, she asked me if I would pray for her as well as give her the Sacrament. I simply asked the Lord if He would bring His healing grace to meet the lady's need. I did not pray for the Lord to heal her blindness. The thought did come to me, but I felt that a little discretion was required. I felt a little nervousness in my spirit and was not sure if it was because I was lacking in faith for the healing of her blindness, or if the Holy Spirit was indicating to me that there was more to this encounter than meets the eye, and a carefully worded prayer was appropriate. However, when I prayed for the Lord to meet her need, I also prayed in my mind for the Lord to heal her blindness. Then, when I reached the end of the row of those kneeling for the Sacrament, I heard a gently sobbing sound. As I looked to my left, the companion was crying as the blind lady had stood up and walked back to her seat unaided. Apparently, some days earlier, whilst in prayer, she felt that the Lord had encouraged her to come to the service at St Catherine's on Holy Wednesday night in the Melin. She wasn't from Neath and had never had anything like such an experience before. That was why, when she came to the altar rail, all she asked for was a prayer and didn't mention healing.

How awesome and mysterious is our Lord and Saviour, Jesus Christ? As I reflected on this healing shortly afterwards, I wondered if the lady would have dared come to the service if the Lord had told her He was going to heal her. Whilst appreciating that an extrovert personality may have been excited at the prospect, this lady seemed quite demur and shy. This incident served to remind me most powerfully that the Lord knows us completely and that knowledge provides the keys to unlocking the ways to communicate with us gently yet profoundly according to our personality and character.

Truly the Lord desires to give us more than we desire or deserve. This is the bedrock of our understanding of what His grace means. Grace is unmerited blessing and favour. The grace of salvation comes to us as a result the sacrificial death of our Lord on the cross. He died that we might not have to die. He destroyed death on the cross and opened to us the gates of heaven. There is nothing we could do to deserve salvation. There is no accumulation of meritorious acts that could result in an individual receiving salvation as a just reward. The grace of salvation is just that – unmerited favour. The only part we have to play in the receiving of such grace is to enter into a living relationship with the author of all heavenly grace – Jesus Christ. The receiving of healing grace flows from the same principles of salvation grace.

All grace is received as unmerited favour from God. In the case of the healing of the Centurion's servant in Luke 7:1-10, the Centurion sent several elders of the Jews to meet with Jesus and ask for Jesus to come and minister healing to the highly valued servant. The elders pleaded with Jesus with the words, *"This man (the Centurion) deserves to have you do this, because he loves our nation and has built our synagogue."* It is impossible to deduce from this that Jesus was so impressed by the plea of the elders that

He decided to set out to heal the servant in order to reward the Centurion for all he had done. It is only as the story unfolds that we understand fully the dynamic of Jesus entering into this situation. Before Jesus arrived at the Centurion's house, friends of the Centurion came to meet Jesus with the message, *"Lord, don't trouble yourself, for I do not deserve to have you come under my roof. That is why I did not even consider myself worthy to come to you. But say the word, and my servant will be healed."* This is the key to the servant being healed by Jesus – the astounding faith of the Centurion. In spite of the Centurion loving the Jewish nation and building their synagogue, he knew he still did not deserve to come to Jesus personally or even have Him in his house. Such humility and faith greatly impressed Jesus and His response was to heal the Centurion's servant. This story serves to illustrate the importance of faith in the context of healing. The faith for healing does not necessarily have to come from the person who is ill. It can come from friends or relatives or a Christian who ministers in the name of Jesus. The next story is an example of the sheer sovereignty of God in healing a young man who lived a godless life in a godless family.

I was about to set off on a Saturday afternoon to watch a rugby match between my home club Cardiff against Neath at the Gnoll in Neath. The telephone rang and I was called into the local hospital in my capacity as the Chaplain. I have to admit I was a little grumpy at the prospect of getting to the game late. In the end, I didn't get there at all. When I arrived at the ward I was escorted to a patient who was unconscious. His mother asked me if I would "do him before he goes". I knew what she meant, but I nevertheless asked her what she wanted me to do. She said, "You know – that Christening thing with the water".

I was about to try a polite refusal and simply offer prayer for her son when I had a sudden check in my spirit as I sensed the Lord prompting me to go ahead. This took me completely off my guard and I asked the mother if she minded me going to the hospital chapel to pray. Her reply was, "Carry on you", as she flicked her wrist in the air with a nonchalance that I found offensive. As I made my way out of the ward, the Sister said that she wanted a word with me. She knew the family, and they were the cause of this eighteen year old making this suicide attempt. She told me that the test results had come back showing that his body had absorbed over three times the lethal dose of barbiturates and he had a very short time to live.

I arrived at the chapel feeling completely at a loss. I protested to the Lord in prayer that it surely was not His prompting in my spirit, but my mind was filled with the words 'DO IT'. I complained that to baptise her son went against all my understanding about baptismal propriety. The young lad was not a Christian and was not asking for baptism. The mother was certainly not a Christian and wanted me to placate her conscience. I felt that I was being used and abused. No way was I going to be a part of such a compromise to my beliefs. But the more I protested, the louder it seemed that the words 'DO IT' came to my mind. In the end, I relented and said I would go ahead with the service in spite of the fact that it went against what I believed to be necessary for a baptism to take place.

On returning to the ward, I found myself saying to the mother that I would go ahead with the service provided I could pray for his recovery before conducting the baptism service. Let me say at this point that I had not resolved to offer prayer for healing as a condition before conducting a baptism service. The words just came from my mouth without any prior thought. Flicking her wrist again she said, "Carry on you". Emotions of anger and confusion came sweeping over me in equal measure. Turning to the young lad in the bed, I anointed him and prayed for his recovery. Then I was taken aback when the doctor present said I would have to leave as the condition of his patient was deteriorating rapidly.

I left the hospital feeling spiritually disorientated and went to my church to just be alone and pray. I confessed to the Lord that I did not know whether I had done right or wrong and I was at a loss to understand anything from the whole incident. I could not process the experience of having the words 'DO IT' fill my mind with such an impact that I had relented and agreed. The feeling of being spiritually in limbo remained with me until I returned to the hospital on the Monday morning.

When I arrived at the ward, the Sister rushed up to me with the heart-stopping greeting, "Steve, it worked! Come and see!" We went into a single room and there he was. The young lad was alive. The Sister explained to me that after I had left, he died and was later transferred to the mortuary. Whilst in the mortuary he sat up and asked where he was. What the mortuary attendant was reputed to have said is not printable. My eyes were filling with tears when I asked him what had happened. He said it seemed as if he was standing on a winding roadway and he saw a figure in the distance who was dressed all in white. The figure moved towards him. The closer the figure came to him, the worse he felt until he simply could not stand. Whilst crouched on the roadway, he felt the impress of a hand on the hair of his head and he heard the words, "My son, it is not time for you to come to Me. Rise, return". On hearing these words, he broke down and wept. There were several parallels between his experience and my own. We had both had a vision of the Lord and heard His voice. Neither of us had done anything consciously to solicit such an experience. Oh, the mercy of God truly knows no bounds. How unutterable awesome is our Lord!

Left to my own devices, if it were not for the Lord's prompting to 'DO IT', I would have refused the mother's request and remained in the comfortable surroundings of my baptism theology feeling proud of myself that I had not compromised. I prayed a prayer of repentance and said to the Lord that I would, from now on, always be prepared to step out of my comfort zones in order to be obedient to Him. If the Lord had asked me to pray for the young lad to be brought back from the dead, I would have been terrified and almost certainly failed to respond. But the Lord knows me altogether and so He simply said 'DO IT'. He knew that I could eventually respond to this. My act of faith was that I was eventually prepared to conduct a baptism service. Then, as I returned to the bedside, the thought came to me to pray for his healing. In so doing, I was being obedient to the prompting of the

Holy Spirit. As I prayed for his healing, I noticed that the tone of my voice was one of authority.

In looking back at this incident I still have a number of questions rumbling in my mind. Why did the Lord want to heal this young lad who had no faith and who came from a family context in which there was no faith? When the Lord told me to 'DO IT', did He really mean that I should baptise the young man or was this a test of my faith that would bring me to a level of faith that I had not experienced before? Was this the level of faith that was necessary for me to be able to minister healing? I had no answer to these questionings and just had to leave it in the realm of the mystery of God. Sometimes I wonder what became of this young man and I pray for him that his life and testimony will bring glory to God.

Shortly after this remarkable healing, I went to a Conference concerning the Holy Spirit and the Gifts of the Spirit. I had a number of misgivings concerning Speaking in Tongues especially, but didn't like to admit it. I had no doubt that it was a genuine Gift of the Holy Spirit and from what I had read, it was a fast growing experience in the Church worldwide. However, I felt very nervous about it because it seemed so 'out of this world' and embarrassing for someone whose comfort zone lay in introversion.

All went well at the Conference until the leaders started speaking about the Baptism in the Holy Spirit and Speaking in Tongues. In truth, I went seeking more information to be able to prayerfully consider the subject. What I did not expect was being put in the situation where the leaders asked each of those attending the conference to indicate if they wanted to be Baptised in the Holy Spirit, and secondly, if we wanted to receive prayer to receive the Gift of Tongues.

My heart started racing as we were asked in turn to give a response to the offer of prayer. Some of those present said that they did not want to be prayed for to receive the Gift of Tongues, but they were all comfortable with being Baptised in the Holy Spirit. When it was my turn to give a response, I was about to decline the offer of being prayed for to receive the Gift of Tongues, when I suddenly, and completely unexpectedly, said in a loud voice that I needed to be Baptised in the Holy Spirit and to receive the Gift of Tongues.

The leaders then prayed for me and although I felt a wonderful sense of peace, I did not speak in 'Tongues'. I genuinely tried but it just didn't seem to happen for me. One of the delegates was a nun who was there as part of her recovery from a nervous breakdown. When she was prayed for, she received the Gift of Tongues immediately and spoke clearly and in a language that seemed to have a wonderfully passionate resonance. Then she burst into tears. She explained that she would have to go back to the Mother House of her Order and tell the Mother Superior what had happened to her. She felt certain the Mother Superior would ask her to leave the Order and the poor nun was in a pitiful state of sorrow and confusion. The leaders of the Conference were superb at this moment and confessed their lack of knowing what to pray for and asked the Holy Spirit to guide them in their prayers. Then they asked us all to pray with confidence for the Lord to resolve the dilemma and do what only He could do. This we did, and then spent considerable time in consoling the nun. I gave her my address and asked her to let me know what happened when she returned to the Convent.

Several weeks later, I received a letter from her that reduced me to tears. When she arrived at the gate of the Convent, there was a nun waiting for her. The nun took her case and told her that the Mother Superior wanted to see her immediately. The Mother Superior told her she felt the Convent would not be the appropriate place for her to be after all. The nun then asked the Mother Superior how it was that she found out what had happened to her at the conference. The Mother Superior said she knew nothing of what happened at the conference and she was referring to something that had happened at the Convent. Apparently, when the nuns were assembled for the service of Compline at the end of the day, they were all chanting when the Holy Spirit came down on them and they all continued chanting in different languages.

They had all received the Gift of Tongues. When the nun enquired when this happened she realised it was at exactly the same time the delegates at the conference were praying for her. The Lord had wonderfully answered our prayers and done what only He could do. We would never have thought for one moment to pray that the Lord would do such a thing. What an awesome God we have!

Little did I know at the time, but the Lord, shortly afterwards, challenged me to put into practice my prayer of being available for His purposes by stepping out of my comfort zones. I was again called in to the hospital. This time it was to baptise a dying baby. When I arrived at the ward, the Sister warned me that the child was severely deformed and to prepare myself emotionally. The parents were either side of their baby and when they turned to meet me the child became visible. I could not control my emotions and the mother hugged me as we all wept. It was one of those moments when the only way to speak was to cry in each other's embraces.

No words could express the emotions and thoughts in those moments. It seemed an age before I could utter a word. The deformities of the poor baby were profound indeed. I conducted the baptism service and prayed that the Lord would take this little one to Himself and restore her in heaven with a perfect resurrection body.

Once more, I went back to my church and knelt at the altar rail weeping and trying to pray. All I could pray over and over again was, "Oh God, oh God, oh God". I just couldn't think of anything else to pray, and confessed to the Lord I was at a loss as to know what to pray. My mind was taken back to the situation in the Conference on the Holy Spirit and the situation that the nun found herself in after she had spoken in 'Tongues'. That seemed an impossible situation and none of us knew at the time what to pray. So I pleaded with the Lord to help me to pray so I would know what He wanted. Then I found myself beginning to pray in 'Tongues' and sensed that I was partnering with God in sorrow for this poor baby. All my misgivings and reticence about Speaking in Tongues were dealt with in this one moment.

However, as I continued to pray in 'Tongues', the sense of sorrow gradually gave way, and my emotion changed.

I now felt a sense of elation and joy that seemed totally inappropriate. I asked the Lord what this meant, but all I got was a clear sense I had to return to the hospital and speak to the mother. When I asked the Lord what it was that He wanted me to say, I was met with total silence. Nothing came to mind at all. Getting back into my car, I asked the Lord to let me know what it was He wanted me to say to the mother. My mind was blank, so I took it to be a challenge to my faithfulness in this situation.

Walking through the hospital car park, I again asked the Lord what it was that He wanted me to say. Again, no thought came to my mind. Walking down the corridor to the ward, I urged the Lord to let me know what to say. Nothing! Not a single thought came into my mind. My heart rate was rising fast. On entering the ward, the mother caught sight of me and the look of surprise on her face made me shout in my spirit for the Lord to let me know what to say. I pleaded with the Lord I had been faithful to the leading of the Holy Spirit and done as I felt I was being led. Still nothing came.

I took a chair and sat beside her. She asked why I had come back. I suddenly felt a surge of authority and assurance as I spoke out. I told her I had been in prayer and that the Lord had told me He was going to take her baby to Himself and that if she would let me pray a prayer of healing for her, then He would heal her, and she would be able to give birth to a perfect baby. She then told me that the Consultant had just been to see her and had told her she would be unable to have any further children. She also told me this was not the first baby that she had given birth to that had had the same congenital deformities. She then said she was puzzled because she could not understand why it was she believed me rather than the Consultant. I found myself saying the Consultant had a Consultant and that His name was the Lord Jesus Christ. She said she was amazed, and could not understand why it was that she believed me. She paused for a moment and looked into my eyes. Her eyes seem to glow with faith and she asked me to pray for her. I prayed and anointed her. I thanked her for giving me the privilege of being allowed to pray for her and duly left.

Again, I went back to the church to just be alone with the Lord and to mull over what had happened in a conversational type of prayer. I told the Lord I was grateful He did not tell me what it was He wanted me to pray for the mother. If He had told me I was to pray for her healing and she would give birth to a child without deformity, then I think all sorts of questions and doubts may have arisen in my mind that could have sapped my faith.

Just over twelve months later I received a letter from her together with a photograph of a beautiful baby. A year later she sent another letter with another photograph. Yet another beautiful baby. The letter contained the news that she had offered herself for Ordination and had been accepted for training.

As I reflected on this experience, I learnt a number of valuable lessons. The first lesson to me was that 'Speaking in Tongues' is such a valuable blessing when in situations of feeling utterly lost for meaningful words in English. I confess that I have so often found myself in this position. There are times when it is just too difficult for me to express my emotions adequately in English, and other times when I am simply stuck as to what to pray for. As an illustration, I am reminded of the Welsh word *'Cariad'*. This word translates as 'darling' or 'dearest' in English. However, an accurate translation of this word would need several sentences. The word speaks of an all-embracing love that involves fidelity in the utmost and a passion that consumes the lover with the loved.

Every language has limitations in what it can express, and so it seems to me that when the Holy Spirit imparts the Gift of Tongues, this new language gift is ideally suited for the individual to be able to express in a different language the inexpressible in the native tongue.

A second lesson was that 'Speaking in Tongues' can be the precursor to receiving the 'Gift of Faith'. This 'Gift of Faith' is not what might be termed faith for salvation. Such faith, for example, may come from a conversion experience or grow gradually over a number of years as a result of being brought up in the Christian faith and living in a Christian environment. Such blessed individuals may never be able to relate a particular conversion experience, but simply know with a surety they belong to Christ and they worship Him in Spirit and in Truth.

The 'Gift of Faith' that I am referring to here is the gift that is noted in 1 Corinthians 12:9 as one of the Gifts of the Spirit. This 'Gift of Faith' may be described as a surge of faith given by the Holy Spirit in situations that call for a ministering profile of faith quite a way beyond the everyday level of a life of faith. In the context described above, when I told the mother that He was going to take the baby to Himself and that if she let me pray for her she would be healed, I was speaking with a sense of authority which was way beyond the normal level of faith conversation.

When the mother told me what the Consultant had said to her, I was experiencing a 'Gift of Faith' for her situation. I was not the least daunted by what she said. In fact I sensed a further rising of authority and faith for her situation. I was speaking with an assurance of certainty that convinced both me and her that we could believe for the outcome of a successful birth. If I had not been experiencing a 'Gift of Faith' at the time then my words would have been words of utter presumptuousness and been cruel in the extreme. My normal level of faith would have been able to believe that the Lord *could* heal her, but the 'Gift of Faith' took me to the level of knowing that the Lord *would* heal her. It is of vital importance to appreciate the difference between the normal level of a living faith and when receiving a 'Gift of Faith', because, to confuse the two can lead to disaster.

Richard Mayhue relates in his book, *Divine Healing Today*, the story of the death of eleven year old Wesley Parker. Wesley's parents took him to their church when a guest preacher held special services including prayers for healing. When the invitation came to receive prayer, Wesley's parents brought him forward. The preacher pronounced Wesley healed of diabetes. A subsequent insulin test showed he had not been healed. Wesley's parents 'claimed' the healing and 'blamed the unexpected insulin results on Satan'. Despite Wesley's deteriorating health, medical attention was withheld. Wesley went into a coma and died.

This incident is a tragic example of what happens when one tries to make a 'law' out of a 'grace'. In other words, it illustrates the truth that you cannot generate in your own mind or spirit the grace of the Gift of Faith. This is spiritual presumptuousness. When the grace of the Gift of Faith is being received, then the outcome is assured. It seems to me the initiation of the Gift of Faith comes from the Holy Spirit and is not generated from within the Christian who is in the situation of a prayer need. In my own experience, I have often prayed to the Holy Spirit for the Gift of Faith for a person or situation. Very rarely has that prayer been answered. When it has been granted, I am aware that my prayer is simply at another level. There is an absolute certainty in my spirit that I am in full partnership with my Lord for the outcome. However, it needs to be stated that I have prayed for many people without experiencing the Gift of Faith operating in my spirit and nevertheless seen the Lord bring the most wonderful healing blessings.

When we look at the list of Spiritual Gifts in 1 Corinthians 12, we note that Paul wrote in 1 Corinthians 12:11 that, *"All these are the work of one and the same Spirit, and he gives to each one, just as he determines."* So it is the Holy Spirit who is the initiator of these Spiritual Gifts. The only exception to this is with regards to the Gift of Tongues. Once received from the Holy Spirit, the Christian may choose to speak or sing in Tongues in private or in public. I have found it a very useful gift to use particularly when I am stuck for what to pray in my native language. To be able to choose to pray in Tongues and then to ask the Holy Spirit for guidance is likened to an antidote to prayerful presumptuousness. There have been many occasions when, having asked someone what would they like me to pray for them, I have been lost as to where to start. Let me illustrate this with an example.

A lady once came for prayer at a Healing Service. When I asked her what it was that she wanted prayer for, she started reciting a supermarket-like shopping list of requests. I asked her if she minded me pausing for a moment whilst I asked for guidance as to where to start. Somewhat disarmingly, she asked me to take all the time I needed. I confessed to the Lord I didn't have the first clue as to where to start and asked Him for guidance. Nothing came to my mind, so I started praying in Tongues.

After a few moments, I had a picture in my mind of a large wooden box with a lock and chain securing the clasp. Around the box were numerous smaller boxes with writing on them that I could not make out. I then asked the lady if her prayer requests were represented by small boxes, what was in the wooden chest. She paused for a moment and tears began to slowly fall from her eyes. She then got up from her knees and slowly walked back to her seat. A short while later she asked if she could see me in private. I agreed and we met in church the following day.

This time she simply wept as she poured out her story of being sexually abused as a young child by her piano teacher who was her uncle. He had threatened her not to tell her parents or anyone else. She confessed that she was an inveterate attention-seeker and that she craved love from people's words of comfort or understanding. However, she cringed at the very thought of physical love. As a consequence of her continuous attention seeking, she could not maintain any long term friendships. I drew her attention to a beautiful verse in 1 Peter 5:7, *"Cast all your anxieties on him because he cares for you."* As I unpacked the meaning of this verse to her, I could see from her eyes a revelation was being given to her. I told her that when problems arrive and we become anxious and fearful, we often tend to share it with others and forget the truth of the verse in 1 Peter that Jesus wants us to share it with Him.

A time of prayer ministry followed in which she forgave the relative concerned and also forgave herself for the guilt that she felt. I then gave her a short prayer format for dealing with the supermarket-like shopping list of prayer requests she had and advised her to use the prayers every day for a month whilst at the same time not mentioning them to anyone else. She agreed to do this and in less than a fortnight came back to me and told me one of her prayer requests had been answered and she had a great sense of peace for the others. What impressed me the most was that she said she did not have the urge to seek people to whom she could pour out her troubles.

6

Honda Wing and a Prayer

The advent of the 1973 oil crisis, when the price of petrol rose dramatically, resulted in me eventually not being able to afford to keep my car. After I sold my car, I decided to buy a Honda 90 motorcycle to be able to get around the parish and attend meetings. There was only one minor complication – I had never ridden a motorcycle before and was extremely nervous.

When the Honda arrived at the house, I put it in the garden and spent the next few days reading the manual. Then the day came for me to give it a go. My nervousness and embarrassment would be hidden by the waterproof clothes and helmet that I bought. I reassured myself with the thought that nobody would know it was me as I was unrecognisable underneath my camouflage of protection. So I walked the contraption to the empty car park of a nearby nursing home. I carefully started the engine and putting the Honda into first gear I rode from one end of the car park to the other. Then I stopped and turned around and went all the way back in first gear. This didn't seem too bad so I decided to do it again and at the halfway point of the car park change into second gear. All seemed nice and easy and I was getting the hang of it very well – or so I thought.

I decided to ride the length of the car park and change into third gear. Mistake. I was so busy concentrating on my gear changes that I didn't notice that the end of the car park was suddenly upon me. The little kerb propelled the Honda into the air and I landed in a field. Unfortunately the field was quite bumpy, so when I landed, my hands went forward which meant that the accelerator was off, but as I ascended the next bump, my hands went forward and the accelerator was engaged and I shot up again. Each unsolicited manoeuvre resulted in the trees in the distance getting ever closer. In the end I was so disorientated and uncoordinated that the only way to stop was to bail out. This I did successfully as I saw my Honda disappear over the next mound.

I was so glad that there was nobody around to watch me. I got to my feet and brushed some of the mud off before retrieving my poor Honda. It was then that I made my second mistake. I was all hot and bothered so I took my helmet off. As I slowly trudged back to the car park, there they were. News must have gone round the nursing home that a deranged incarnation of Evel Knievel had arrived at their car park to provide the evening's entertainment. Not only that, but two of the residents recognised me and opened their widows to give me a round of applause. I paused, gave them a polite bow, and then made my crestfallen way back home. When I got to the back door, Marilyn made me take all my outer clothes off before I was allowed in. When I told her what had happened, she was extremely sympathetic. In between wiping the tears from her eyes with laughter she offered a question full of insight and practical wisdom and asked, "Which parish shall we go to next?" It was at that time that I entered into the hilarity of the debacle.

The following evening, I resolved to try again but go to a different place. This time I went to a street that had the same entrance and exit. It was a large horseshoe street and with no through traffic it promised to be more of a sedate exercise for me and my Honda. I walked the Honda to the entrance of the road and was grateful to notice that all was quiet. Off I went in first gear and then changed to second gear when all of a sudden a rabid canine of monstrous proportions came bounding out of a driveway. I quickly assessed the situation and came to the conclusion that this was not a friendly animal coming to give me a good licking. It was all teeth with a murderous intent and so I took a deep breath and panicked.

I couldn't trust myself to change smoothly into third gear and turned the accelerator on as far as it would go whilst remaining in second gear. The noise from my screaming engine was appalling as the monster canine gradually gained on me. I kept looking in my rear view mirror and didn't pay a great deal of attention as to where I was going. I breathed a huge sigh of relief as I saw the dog losing ground as it ran out of vitriolic steam. Then I looked up and to my horror there in front of me was a gang of four frenzied dogs coming towards me. I remember shouting out, "My God, open the Pearly Gates, I'm on my way!" As the moment of encounter was quickly approaching, I changed into third gear and closed my eyes driving straight through them. Thank the Lord that I didn't hit any of them. When I got home, Marilyn asked me what had happened, as I was ashen. Again I told her of my near death experience and had the full sympathy treatment again. She couldn't talk for laughing and crying.

The following day I had an appointment with an elderly parishioner to give her Communion in her house. On arrival she said that she had something to tell me. She said that the previous evening she heard a cacophony of noise coming down the street and she went to her window to see what the commotion was about. "You'll never guess what I saw. There was a lunatic on a motor bike being chased by a dog. We haven't seen him before and we hope that we never see him again." I nearly choked and pretended to cough so as to give myself enough time to compose myself. It was all I could do to not tell her that the lunatic was about to give her Communion.

Marilyn, being a vicar's wife, was dedicated to a life of discretion and propriety and as such she would never divulge anything that might compromise my status as a leading member of the community. And so I went to church the following Sunday thinking that the incidents were a matter of the past. How wrong I was. Marilyn had told the organist, and the opening hymn that was chosen was *Onward Christian Soldiers*. Not only had she told the organist, but when I was in the vestry getting ready for the service, she told the entire congregation and so when the hymn began, everyone sang, "Honda Christian soldiers…" To add insult to injury, the final hymn was *Oh God Forgive Our Foolish Ways*.

Whilst at Neath, my wife Marilyn gave birth to our second child, Emma on May 29th 1975.

Letters From Bishop Eryl Thomas

As a result of the healings that were taking place during my time in Neath, I felt it was right to make contact with Bishop Eryl Thomas. I was convinced the Ministry of Healing was a ministry that had largely been put to one side in the Anglican Church and the Lord wanted it to be reinstated as an essential and vital part of the Gospel presentation. It was with some trepidation I met the Bishop. I had no idea how he would receive what had been happening at Neath and how he would react to my suggestion, as a mere Curate, that I felt called by God to play a part in enabling the Church to rediscover the Ministry of Healing. However, I need not have been so concerned because the Ministry of Healing was already on the agenda of the Church in Wales as the Bishop explained. Indeed, he was elated at the healings that were taking place and asked me to keep him informed on a regular basis. I followed up our meeting with a letter and the Bishop's reply gave me great encouragement to press on and to grow into a greater understanding and ministry credibility. The following is an extract from that letter dated 6th January 1975,

> "My dear Steve, Thank you for your letter of 20th December. I have given much thought to the aims and objectives of your present group in the light of what you were able to tell me when we last met, and also to the wider question of the expansion of the normal sacramental Ministry of Healing in the parishes.

> "As you know, I am to meet with you and two or three others early in February to discuss how this can best be done. I believe that the only way is to get regional groups of people concerned about the Church's Ministry of Healing who could then form cells of

prayer groups in parishes and gradually come to instruct other people in the work of healing. Those who belong to your group would be useful spearheads in the different regions.

"We had a Provincial Consultation about this at Aberystwyth over a year ago and I think Norman Autton has been following this up in the different Dioceses so that groups of clergy and laity are being formed either in the Deanery or Parish or wider region.

"My own feeling about your group is that it should continue to be something quite independent, concerned with healing but also with the current Charismatic Movements in the Church today. I would hope that you will still allow me to meet the group, and that any meeting that you arranged with a special speaker of some note and authority should be given wide publicity either through the Diocesan Leaflet or by letter to incumbents, or possibly through Rural Deans. It is important that everyone should have the chance of hearing about what is going on not only further afield but locally, and where the potential might lie in the future. There is so much that could come out of this which could capture the uncommitted young person for the Christian Faith.

"I am anxious to further any movement that is for the good of the Christian Faith, and there are very many channels through which the Holy Spirit is at work today."

Not long after writing this letter, tragedy struck. Bishop Eryl committed a grave indiscretion and as a result he had to resign as the Bishop of Llandaff. The whole of the Church in Wales reeled at the news. Bishop Eryl had commanded the greatest of respect as a strong and vibrant leader in the Church. He spoke with a natural and not overbearing authority that solicited the listening ear. It was a tremendous shame that his vision and dynamism came to a premature end. I wrote to him to express my deep sadness at the news and he invited me to come and visit him and his wife Jean. The following is an extract of his letter in reply,

"You and I have been too closely aligned in so many aspects of our work together for a disastrous downfall to separate us altogether. You may not have realised how greatly I admired your ministry and the courageous way in which you persevered in reopening channels of healing grace when so often those who ought to have rejoiced with you in your convictions preferred to pour cold water on your ventures. Similarly your witness in bringing into prominence once again the best gifts of the Charismatic Movement, founded in personal prayer and the element of sacrifice, has in my opinion sown the seeds of much potential good for the future. So dear Steve, press on and fulfil your ministry undeterred by my failure.

"The breaking points in our life are mysterious and inexplicable, but it is particularly sad when they come at the end of a life in which grace had until then triumphed.

"God bless you in your days ahead and make you a sharp instrument in His service."

When I went to visit Bishop Eryl and Jean, it was with a heavy heart that I found them both very subdued. We had tea together and managed to laugh as we recalled several of the humorous incidents that we shared when I was a curate at Llandaff Cathedral. Towards the end of our time together, I finally plucked up enough courage to ask if I could pray for them. They readily agreed and said they were looking forward to it immensely. Being freed from the shackles of a spirit of timidity, I prayed for the blessing of the grace of forgiveness and for healing in their relationship and in their personal lives. It was a very precious and tearful time and an immense privilege to be able to come alongside them as a friend whose love for them never wavered.

True friends are those who make it their business to come alongside those who have fallen foul of temptation. Surely we have the mandate from Our Lord to hate sin but love the sinner? Didn't Jesus eat and drink and associate with sinners? He wasn't afraid of losing His reputation from onlookers by associating with sinners. He was concerned to please His Heavenly Father by going after the lost sheep and giving the message of the Kingdom of God to all who would listen. He set an example for us to follow. We will *'share His sufferings'* if we follow that example and we too will be misunderstood and misrepresented by those who choose to tread safely in the courts of the so-called socially respectable. I write this because one of my colleagues asked me if I realised the risk that I was taking if it became widely known that I had visited Bishop Eryl and his wife. I have always found that such safety first ministry is spiritually anaemic and devoid of the divine compassion for all mankind that necessitated the Incarnation.

Healing, Heartache and Humour

7

Our Arrival at Cyfarthfa Church

In 1977, I went to see the Bishop of Llandaff the Rt Rev John Poole-Hughes with a view to discerning my next appointment. I explained to him that I would prefer to be sent to a parish that was impoverished and had a significant number of marginalised and sick people. He suggested that I should consider the parish of Bedlinog and an appointment was made for me to visit the area together with the Rural Dean, the Rev Michael Short.

On the day of the visit, Marilyn could not come with me as the children were not very well. Whilst driving from Neath to Bedlinog, I went through Merthyr Tydfil and sensed a warming in my spirit. By the time I met with Rev Michael Short at the church in Bedlinog, the feeling had gone. Michael showed me around the parish and we met with a number of parishioners who were warm and friendly. The parish ticked all the boxes for me but I could not let go of the experience I had when I travelled through Merthyr Tydfil. At the end of the visit, I told Michael that I did not have a sense of calling to Bedlinog. He replied that there was only one other vacancy in his area and that was in the parish of Merthyr Tydfil. He explained that the Rectorial Benefice of Merthyr Tydfil did not have anyone to lead the congregation at Cyfarthfa Church. He went on to say that I would probably not be interested in the post as a vicar in a Rectorial Benefice because vicars in Rectorial Benefices were in reality curates, whereas I had been sent by the bishop to look at a parish needing a vicar. I asked if I could visit the Rectorial Benefice and be shown around.

Arrangements were made for Marilyn, Sarah and Emma and myself to have an informal look at the area first before committing to a formal visit. It was a lovely sunny day so we decided to take a picnic lunch with us. We drove around, praying as we went that we would be given a clear discernment if this was where the Lord wanted us to go. And clear discernment we certainly got. Parking the car outside the vicarage, we opened the large iron gates and taking our picnic with us, laid out a blanket on the grass. We sat in a little circle and out came the ham rolls, crisps, sausages, drinks and cakes. Then, without warning, we were startled to hear a voice shout out, "What are you doing in there?" The elderly figure was holding on to the iron gate with head pressed against the bars. It was Mary Price, one of the elderly members of the Cyfarthfa Church congregation.

I explained that I was a priest and that I was looking at the parish with a view to applying for the vacancy. Her reply made us laugh when she said, "Oooooh vicar, you'll find that we are a real family church. Don't you worry about a thing, we'll all look after you. Now you enjoy your picnic and I'll just let everybody know the good news." Before I could say that we were only just looking at the parish and had not made up our minds, she speedily disappeared. Somewhat amused by this encounter, we settled down to our picnic when out of nowhere a rather scrawny and emaciated chicken arrived and stood by Marilyn. Then three more arrived and they proceeded to run around us in a scene that was reminiscent of a cowboy movie where the Indians encircle a wagon train. Around and around they went making the most dreadful noise as they did so. Suddenly one of them broke ranks and dived in between us, grabbing the ham roll that Emma was about to put into her mouth. Now we were under all out attack from these SAS (Snatch All Sausages) trained birds so I grabbed the four corners of the blanket and we all made a hasty retreat to the safety of our car. The crazed chickens disappeared as fast as they arrived and we later found out they had been left by the previous occupant to fend for themselves! In spite of the chickens, we really sensed this was where the Lord wanted us to be and the welcome of Mary Price was most certainly instrumental in our decision to make a formal visit to the parish.

After I had made the decision to accept the position of the Vicar of Cyfarthfa Church in the Rectorial Benefice of Merthyr Tydfil and Cyfarthfa, Marilyn and I were shown around the parish by Jim Payne, one of the Church Wardens. Jim had a terrible affliction. He was a lifelong supporter of Cardiff City, an affliction I shared with him. We immediately took to Jim and our families enjoyed many happy times together. Jim's wife, Margaret, was a lady of great faith and a long suffering wife who endured with much grace the endless stream of Irish jokes that Jim would reel off at the drop of a hat.

My first day of parochial visiting was memorable indeed. I decided to see the two postmasters in the parish. At Heolgerrig Post Office, I met Mr Thomas and his son. They were very welcoming and eager to tell me the latest local story. Apparently they had just been visited by a man who worked for the Provident company and had come back from collecting money in the Gurnos Estate. When he returned to his car which he had parked on the estate, the Provident man noticed that the near side rear tyre of his car was flat, so he opened the boot and took out the jack to change the wheel. When it was raised high enough, he took out the spare wheel but noticed the car was still rocking slightly. On lowering the boot lid, he saw someone in the front of his car in the process of taking out the radio. He shouted at the young man and asked him what on earth he was doing. The young man replied that being as he was having the wheels, he thought he would have the radio! On hearing this story, I began to wonder what sort of place I had come to. I needn't have been concerned because in due course of time I met some wonderful people in the Gurnos and realised it had gained a largely unwarranted reputation.

The second Post Office was in the Gellideg Estate. Once again, I was warmly welcomed by Mr Cook, the Postmaster. He described the area and the issues it was facing. There was one person, nicknamed Bobo, who lived on the estate and described by Mr Cook as the local villain. He said that Bobo made Al Capone look like Andy Pandy in comparison. Suddenly, Mr Cook froze behind the counter screen. I asked what was the matter. He said that whatever I did, I was not to turn round. Why is it that when someone says that to you, there is an instinct to turn round? As I turned round I asked again what was the matter. Mr Cook said that Bobo had just come into the Post Office. The instant that Bobo saw my dog collar, he called me over to talk to him. My heart was in my mouth. He said that he had decided that he was going to heaven. I answered that getting people to heaven was my job and asked him what had brought him to that conclusion. He answered he believed the devil was a canny b….. and if the devil let him into hell, he was so evil he knew he would have his job within two weeks. I laughed nervously and he placed a hand on my shoulder and said, "Well done, Vic, you'll do for me." As I left the Post Office, again I wondered what on earth I had come to.

Some years later, Bobo came to visit me after the vicarage had been burgled. He said he had made it his business to discover the name of the culprit. Successful in his search, he had come to give me a special offer. The price was £200 for a leg and £100 for an arm. The first limb would be free but I would have to pay for any further retribution. I explained how grateful I was to receive such a generous offer but on this occasion I felt that I must decline. As he left he said that if ever I changed my mind then I just had to contact him. On closing the door, I had the flash of a mental image of headlines in the local newspaper the *Merthyr Express*, "Vicar hires hitman".

Years later, I met Bobo in town and he told me that he had just become a Christian for real. He'd gone to a mid-week Christian meeting and had a conversion experience. With tears in his eyes, he said that it had turned his world upside down. He then asked me if I would take his funeral on the occasion of his death. When I agreed, he told me to preach the Gospel but to use humour. He felt that if I used humour to illustrate the Gospel then the congregation would listen.

Two weeks later Bobo died. Having been admitted to Prince Charles Hospital, he gave his occupation as 'Retired Cowboy'. I remember the night before the funeral as one of wrestling with my sermon. In the end, I decided to make up a story. Bobo regularly visited Margam Park in the dead of night to hunt for deer. He would cut it up and give much of it away whilst selling the remainder as 'rich Welsh lamb'.

I began the service at Llwydcoed Crematorium by introducing myself and asking the congregation if they knew that Bobo's full nickname was 'Bobo, The Paper Bag Kid'. Members of the congregation began muttering amongst themselves and one was heard to say, "What is that vicar on?"

Then I told the story that I had concocted about a bounty hunter going into the Sheriff's office and asking him if there were any wanted men in the area. The Sheriff opened his drawer and pulled out a wanted poster. It was a poster of Jesse James who was wanted dead or alive and the bounty for him was $10,000. The bounty hunter was impressed but asked if there were any wanted men in the area who were worth more. The Sheriff brought out another poster, this time for Billy the Kid who was wanted dead or alive for a bounty of $20,000. The bounty hunter was again impressed, but asked who was the most wanted man in the area. The Sheriff told him it was Bobo, The Paper Bag Kid and there was a $100,000 reward for his capture. The bounty hunter said that he would go after Bobo, but before he left the office he asked the Sheriff why Bobo was called The Paper Bag Kid. The Sheriff explained that Bobo had a paper bag for a hat, a huge paper bag with slits cut into it for a shirt, another huge paper bag with a slit for his waist and cut down the middle to make the trousers, and paper bags for his shoes. The bounty hunter was totally confused by this explanation and asked the Sheriff what on earth he was wanted for. The Sheriff replied, "RUSTLING!"

At that, the congregation dissolved into laughter and I heard a shriek coming from the organist behind me. I went on to explain there is a bounty on all of our heads because we have all sinned and there is a price to be paid. The only way to escape paying the ultimate price for our sin is if someone else pays the price for us. Jesus is the only one who claims to have paid the price for our sin, but we must repent and accept His free gift of salvation.

At the end of the service, when everyone had left, I went to see the organist to find out why she had let out a shriek. She said that she would never forgive me. She knew Bobo's reputation, and when I told the story about the Bounty Hunter and the Sheriff she wet herself so much so that she was afraid to use the pedals of the organ for the last hymn. I guess you can't please everybody all of the time, but I am sure that Bobo would have approved of the story!

The third visit that I made on my first day was to Peggy and Tudor Rowlands. Peggy had been a faithful member of the church for many years and was on the Parochial Church Council – the leadership team. She was suffering from phlebitis and was finding it difficult to walk and also tend for her husband Tudor who was in a bed downstairs as he had had a leg amputated.

Tudor's faith had taken a severe blow and at this time he did not seem at all interested in my faith story. I asked Peggy if I could pray for her. I took this as an opportunity to share testimonies of healing so as to encourage faith in Peggy for when I prayed, and also for Tudor to hear so as to give him the opportunity of reconnecting with the faith that he had lost.

As I prayed for Peggy, she felt an unusual heat in her legs. She asked if this meant she was being healed and I told her that it did. In the evening she rang me to tell me that all the swellings had gone down and she was completely healed. When I returned to their house the following day, Tudor had been so surprised and taken aback by the healing Peggy had received that he began asking questions about Christianity and I could tell he really wanted to regain his faith. A short while later, he asked if he could receive Holy Communion at home. I was delighted to do this and subsequently went to the house each month to give him the Sacrament. His faith continued to grow in spite of the fact he had been told he had to have his second leg amputated. I had prayed for his healing and anointed him, but his physical condition continued to deteriorate. The time came for him to be admitted to the local Prince Charles Hospital and his condition soon became critical. When visiting him, he asked many questions about death and heaven. I have to admit I felt inadequate in most of the explanations I gave him and I told him so. With a calm and assured faith he said it didn't really matter as he would soon find out all the answers for himself. I asked him if he would put in a good word for me when he got to heaven. He said he would ask God to give me more of whatever it takes to become more effective in the healing ministry. It was a lovely moment when, stripped of all the usual pretence and denial, we were able to speak almost casually about his impending death.

I left the hospital feeling quite elated and returned to the vicarage where Marilyn had invited a few friends for the afternoon. As we were sat in the lounge, I suddenly heard what I thought at first to be the music sound of an ice cream van approaching. I asked everyone if they could hear an ice cream van nearby. They all said that they couldn't. Then the sound grew louder and louder and it seemed as if there was an incredible peel of bells ringing. I knew in my spirit what this was. Tudor had just been taken to heaven. I excused myself and said that I needed to make a phone call. I rang the hospital ward and the Sister told me that Tudor had just passed away. After putting the phone down, I reflected on what an outstanding privilege it was to be able to minister the Gospel and the grace of God. To journey with Tudor and see him come back to faith was a great joy. To prepare him to meet His Lord and Saviour was the consummation of that joy.

As I continued to minister at Cyfarthfa Church, there were a number of matters that had to be addressed if the church was going to be able to grow into a family of spiritual significance.

The first issue which had to be dealt with was that of fundraising. The amount of work that went into raising money through sales of work, garden fetes, raffles and the like, was considerable. Many of these events attracted non Church members to attend and give their financial support. But these events were not evangelistic and bore little or no fruit with regards to increasing the Faith community. It wasn't that the congregation were unspiritual, rather it was a case of maintaining the status quo with regards to presenting the Church to the community.

I made a presentation to the leadership team to stop all fund-raising events and choose to survive on the financial giving of the members only. It seemed to me that to rely on non-Church members to support the ongoing work of the Church was not pleasing to the Lord. It would take an act of faith to do this as without that support the Church would not be able to maintain its financial commitments. To my delight, the motion was passed. We still had social evenings and occasions when non Church members were invited to events, but these were not for the purpose of raising money. Teaching on tithing quickly followed and very soon the Church finances increased considerably. I put together a three year course on the reasons to tithe time, talents and money and integrated it into the teaching plan for the Church. As a consequence, we were informed after a few years that the giving per capita at the Church was higher than any other Anglican Church in Wales. Years later I was asked to present this course to a Provincial Stewardship Committee. A Stewardship Officer told me afterwards that although the course would fit into any kind of Churchmanship, it was regarded by the clergy on the committee as far too challenging and something that they could never sell to their congregations. I found this very sad because the course easily lent itself to be adapted to fit a variety of parish profiles.

One of the features that caused a measure of consternation was to do with how a parish relates to the great Missionary Societies such as the Church Missionary Society, the United Society for the Propagation of the Gospel and the South American Missionary Society. There was no doubting the fact that these and other Missionary Societies serve the Church very well and do extremely valuable work worldwide, but they do this work *on behalf of* the parishes. One of the effects of this is that the parishes often develop a mindset that they are engaged in overseas Mission through the fundraising and/or donations from the collections of the Churches. In itself, this is not a problem, but it does become a problem when such support abrogates the responsibility for personal involvement in overseas Mission. We struggled with this issue at Cyfarthfa Church for several years.

A large part of our Missionary Giving went to the three Societies mentioned above. However, we gradually introduced into the parish calendar opportunities for ministering abroad. Together with another local church, a number of our members went to Satu Mare in Romania. A convoy of vehicles took medical supplies, food and clothing to the beleaguered town. The welcome that was given to those who went was overwhelming and life-changing. They met Pastor Zoltan, the leader of a local church and kept in touch with him for many years. The difference in the congregation's attitude to Overseas Mission was palpable as the group shared their testimonies in Church and Home Groups. The appetite for Overseas Mission grew and we took up further opportunities that presented themselves to be involved in Kenya and Mozambique.

Heddwyn Williams had been a missionary for the Church Missionary Society and when he left the Society, he founded the 'Children of Hope' mission in Nairobi, Kenya together with his wife Lydia. Their passion was to reunite street children with their families or to help them to be adopted. Heddwyn's family home was in Swansea, so when he visited his home he and Lydia, sometimes with their children, would come to give us an update on their work. They always inspired us with their prayerfulness in the face of many difficulties and their sheer joy was deeply humbling.

Ted Rowlands was our Member of Parliament and also a member of Cyfarthfa Church. When he was at the Foreign Office, he formed a friendship with Samora Michel, the President of Mozambique. Ted had been invited by the President to see for himself the dire situation that existed in Mozambique. He had recently heard that after many years of drought, the country had experienced such a deluge of water that there was utter devastation everywhere. He spoke at a Church service before he went, explaining what had happened in the country and asking for our prayers and support. When he returned, he was in a very solemn mood. Holding back the tears, he eloquently described what he had seen and heard. For example, he had taken a boat ride on the flood waters and heard the cry of a baby. Looking up, he saw a tree and a mother holding a baby. The mother had died but the baby was still alive.

After giving his report, the Church worked with Ted and together we were determined to make a difference. We set up a collection throughout the entire Borough of Merthyr Tydfil to raise funds so as to purchase specialist irrigation pumps from a company in Dursley, Gloucestershire. Ted even took up a collection in the Foreign Office in London. We purchased six pumps and enough spare parts to last twenty years. The equipment was shipped to Mozambique at no cost to the fund and the consignment was met at the docks in the capital Maputo by the British Ambassador and the local Bishop, Dinis Sengulane. The pumps were taken to the most fertile area in Mozambique, the Chokwe District.

In the years that followed we received several reports that the pumps were doing their work and that many lives had been saved as a result. Cyfarthfa Church then provided the funds for twenty missionaries to be trained in Maputo. The country was in Communist control and it was with great joy that we learnt of the success of these missionaries as many people were converted. As a thank you to Cyfarthfa Church and the people of the Borough of Merthyr Tydfil, the Communist leader of the Chokwe District allowed us to provide for the building of a Church in his District. It only cost a few hundred pounds but it represented the start of an indigenous missionary endeavour which proved very successful. One of the consequences of such engagement with overseas mission was that the collections from our members increased. People had been provided with a reason to give and they responded wonderfully.

When Bishop Dinis Sengulane came to visit Cyfarthfa Church, there was a great celebration. He was such a blessing. He was small of stature but hugely impressive in his persona. Faith and love seemed to cascade from his eyes. He spoke with the kind of authority and gravitas that could only be forged on the anvil of faith in adversity.

As he addressed the congregation concerning the situation in Mozambique, we were deeply moved. Mozambique at that time was the poorest nation in the world in terms of its economy. The infrastructure was desperately fractured and fragmented. Food production had been at an all-time low and many people were starving from the drought that had lasted for a number of years. Prayers were prayed that the Lord might send rain so that crops could be grown. When the rain eventually fell, there was massive flooding over a great area. Even the crops that were growing at the time were destroyed. The Bishop explained how he led the Church in his Diocese not only to grapple with the inevitable question as to why God should have allowed this tragedy to happen, but how to respond to the tragedy with faith and hope.

A number of people in the congregation became quite tearful when he said that if the tragedy had not happened then Ted Rowlands would not have visited him, and the specialist irrigation pumps that we were able to purchase would never have been bought. He went on to say that many thousands of lives had been saved as a consequence of what the people in the Borough had provided. He then redirected the attention of the congregation from Mozambique to Merthyr Tydfil, by stating that we could also learn the very important lesson that when Christians pray and things seem to get worse rather than better, some fall away and stop praying, whilst others pray even more fervently in the sure and certain hope that our God is a God of love, and in His inscrutable wisdom and timing there will be blessings and answers that will come at a future time. The passion that was conveyed in his words clearly came from a man who had practiced what he had preached in the most extreme of circumstances.

The third issue that needed to be addressed was the most important. The congregation had no concept of the gifts and ministries of the Holy Spirit. Although many of my experiences thus far had included this key area of teaching, I had not been in the context where significant instruction had been appropriate. My ministries at Llanharan, the Cathedral and Neath, were all short term appointments whereas here at Cyfarthfa Church, I knew it would be for the long term. I believed that in order to lead a parish into an Evangelical and Charismatic model of what Church could be, then it would take considerable time and effort. I also knew I did not have the personal qualifications or experience necessary to accomplish the task. I needed a great deal more personal ministry and training.

There is always the temptation to minister out of the puddle of what we have come to know and understand, but I was determined that I wanted to minister out of the ocean of what is available through the gifts and ministries of the Holy Spirit. In order to lay a solid foundation for in-depth teaching on the person and work of the Holy Spirit, I provided teaching notes on how to have a Quiet Time with the Lord. Members were encouraged to use the notes in their private devotions so as to deepen their faith and develop a more profound and personal relationship with the Lord. Alongside these teaching notes, I felt that it was necessary to forge a link with a missionary endeavour that could bring both teaching and personal ministry to myself and the leaders in our church.

To this end, I read many books on Charismatic Renewal and was much impressed by *When the Spirit Comes* written by Colin Urquhart. Colin resigned from his post as vicar of St Hugh's, in Lewsey, Luton, in 1976 and founded Kingdom Faith Ministries based at The Hyde in Sussex. It was this ministry that provided the ideal resource I had been searching for. Over a period of time, most of our members who were in leadership attended Kingdom Faith events. Together, we learnt and experienced so much about the gifts and ministries of the Holy Spirit, and we developed a glorious relationship of friendship and fellowship that resulted in a critical mass being formed for the spiritual renewal of the congregation to take place.

8

Thrown in at the Deep End - And Found Wanting

A few months after arriving at Cyfarthfa Church, I led the worship group at an Anglican Renewal Conference in Aberystwyth University. The main speaker was Roy Peacock. Roy spoke regularly at meetings of the Full Gospel Businessman's International. It was such an encouragement to be so close to someone who was both profound in his teaching and powerful in ministry. When he prayed for people, most fell down as the power and presence of the Holy Spirit touched them. There were numerous testimonies of people who had received spiritual and physical breakthroughs. I confess that I was more than a little nervous at seeing so many bodies on the floor. But I was safe. I was leading the worship group, so I could observe from a safe distance. Or so I thought.

At the last session of the conference, the hall was packed with hundreds of people and after Roy had spoken, he turned to me and asked if the worship group could play without me. I nervously replied that they could. He then said there were far too many people present for him to minister to on his own and asked me to assist. He said that there were to be two lines of people, one going to him and the other going to me. I could literally feel the adrenaline coursing through me. I felt completely out of my depth and in the midst of a crisis of competence. Surely all those who were in the line going to Roy would fall down and those who were in my line would remain ramrod straight. Yes, I had prayed with people before this and witnessed a number of blessings being received, but this was something else.

As the lines of people began to form all I could pray was, "Oh God", as my heart pounded with trepidation. Then the worship group began to play and people started to move forward for prayer. A middle aged couple came towards me and I asked them what I should pray for. The man faltered, "I,I,I,I,I,I," and to my total astonishment the two of them fell down. Then Roy turned to me and said, "How did you do that?" I immediately began to ingratiate myself as a surge of pride swept over me. For a moment I felt ten feet tall. Then the reality of my reaction hit me. I quickly asked the Lord to forgive me and, as I did, I caught sight of a man standing in the doorway of the hall. He was staring at me.

The ministry time continued and there were bodies everywhere on the floor. It was an outstanding moment for me, but I was annoyed with myself for my initial reaction of personal pride. The man at the door did not come forward for prayer. He just stood there all the time, leaning in the doorway and fixing his gaze on me. I felt distinctly uncomfortable.

At the close of the meeting, people began to leave, but he remained in the doorway. There was no other way out. I tried to pretend that I hadn't noticed him as I walked passed. He said, "Excuse me", as I came alongside him. I turned and then he said, "You're in trouble, aren't you?" I surprised myself with my reaction. I found myself saying, "Yes. How did you know?" He then told me what he thought that the Lord had given him concerning me. The Words of Knowledge he was given made me feel I was back at that service in Hounslow. The words were specific and accurate. I asked him who he was and he said his name was the Rev Trevor Blackshaw and that he was in leadership with a group called Wholeness Through Christ. He invited me to visit him at his parish in Mid Wales.

When I got back from the conference, I telephoned Trevor and made arrangements to visit him and his wife Pamela. In the meantime, I learnt a most valuable lesson the hard way. When praying for people, I used to alternate between closing my eyes and opening them. It's amazing how ingrained it is to close one's eyes whilst praying. I think it often traces back to the time when I was in school. The teachers leading Assembly used to say, "Now children, we are going to pray, so hands together and eyes closed." I remember once being sent out of Assembly because I was caught with my eyes open.

Anyway, when I got back from the conference, a member of the church asked for prayer after the morning service. We were standing by the choir stalls and, with eyes closed, I prayed that the Lord would take him into a deeper relationship with Him. This was what he had asked for and this is what he got, but not in the way that I had imagined. When I opened my eyes he had disappeared, at least this was what I thought had happened for a fleeting moment until I looked at his prostrate body on the carpet. My first thought was that of being grateful he had fallen on the soft carpet and had come to no harm. He remained there for several minutes with a huge smile on his face. Then he opened his eyes and asked what had happened to him. I explained that there are times when we are prayed for in which we receive such an experience of the presence of God that we lose all bodily strength for a while and in that time the Lord is blessing us at a most profound level. He was quite wobbly when he got on his feet and had to sit down for a while before he regained normal strength.

Shortly afterwards a church member asked if he could receive ministry in church. It was a mid-week lunchtime. When he arrived, he opened his heart and shared something of the desperation he was feeling. How dull can you get? I closed my eyes yet again and began to pray for him whilst standing behind him just in case he fell. How dull was that? If he fell backwards and I had my eyes closed we would probably both have fallen. In the event, he didn't fall backwards, he fell forwards. He hit his forehead on the uncarpeted stone step leading to the altar. The sound was exactly the same as that of a coconut being hit by a wooded ball at a fairground. As he lay motionless on the floor, I honestly thought he was dead. Kneeling beside him quickly I could see he was still breathing, but what amazed me was that there wasn't a mark on his head. He lay there for over half an hour. Then he opened his eyes and began to tell of a wonderful experience he had had. I asked him if he would be so kind as to hold his head and press gently all around it. He queried this and asked the reason why. When I told him what had happened, he felt all around his head and said he had no pain whatsoever. I had read about similar experiences happening when people fell down during prayer ministry times, and that although they sometime hit themselves on chairs and other obstacles nearby, they came to no harm, but I confess it scared the living daylights out of me. I subsequently learned that there numerous visible signs when the Holy Spirit begins ministering to a person – all of which will be missed if the person ministering has his or her eyes shut.

When I visited Trevor and his wife Pamela, they welcomed me to their home and explained to me what the Wholeness Through Christ ministry was all about. This was indeed a 'divine appointment'. I welcomed their offer to attend a course with open arms. They explained to me what the process would be, and that, on the course, many of my deepest hurts and wounds would be identified and addressed. I felt at ease and confident it would be a life-changing conference and so it proved to be.

The first few days concentrated on teaching about the healing of memories together with lovely times of worship and prayer. The sense of being in the presence of God increased as the days went by and everyone grew quite close together. It seemed as if we had known each other for years and the sharing of personal stories and issues in our lives naturally flowed in conversation. Amidst all our problems and challenges, we found ourselves in an oasis of peace and safety. Then the time came for each one of us to have a personal ministry time. When one of us was being prayed for in a separate room, the rest of us gathered in the large common room to pray. We were encouraged to pray and worship, interspersed with times of silence. The appointed leader of the group took notes on the words of knowledge, prophecy, and Scriptures that were deemed to be relevant for the person being prayed for. These notes were then given to the members of the Wholeness Through Christ team to be confirmed as relevant and appropriate to the lives of those who were receiving prayer ministry. The detail of some of the words of knowledge was truly outstanding. The dynamic of what was happening in the common room was awesome and a little difficult to accurately describe. It was as if the Lord was letting us in on a number of issues that were being prayed through in the individual prayer room so that we could intercede powerfully with heartfelt compassion and love.

When I was being prayed for, the group in the common room were receiving words of knowledge and prophecy about me which I was later given. There were three specific words of knowledge that I recall. The Holy Spirit had revealed to them that when my mother was three months pregnant with me, my father left her for another woman. It was as specific as that. This was the same word of knowledge given to the couple who prayed for me at the Hounslow conference years earlier. Another of the Words of Knowledge was of a boy dressed up in an Indian costume who was on fire. This incident happened to me just as they were shown. I was dressed in a Red Indian outfit and stood too close to a small fire that we made in the woods near our home. As my trousers caught fire, I just stood there, not putting the flames out. My friends saw this and knocked me to the ground and put the flames out. The instinct for survival was just not in me.

Another word of knowledge that the group received about me was of a pack of dogs running towards me and I was just standing there, not running away. Again, this was true. It took place a short while after the fire incident. I was in the woods on my own when I heard the sound of dogs running through the autumn leaves that lay thick on the ground. When I turned, they were making straight for me. I just stood there and the dogs knocked me over. The instinct to push them away just did not happen. Then, all of a sudden a man appeared from behind a tree and he shouted at the dogs, "Go!" At the sound of his voice the dogs ran off. When I got to my feet, the man had disappeared. Who was he? Looking back, I now think it was almost certainly an angel. I can't imagine a pack of dogs running away at the sound of that one word unless my rescuer was not of human origin.

These Words of Knowledge were just three of several that were being prayed through by the Wholeness Through Christ ministers during my private appointment with them. My appointment lasted over three hours, but there were others that took even longer. At the end of the conference we were given profound teaching on the subject of 'How to Walk out Your Healing'. This teaching proved invaluable and has subsequently been a blessing to many people with whom I have had the privilege of praying. I was invited to attend another three Prayer Schools, spanning two years, so that I could receive further personal ministry and training.

It was at one of the Wholeness Through Christ Prayer Schools that I met the Rev John Bedford, who was the pastor at Brandhall Baptist Church in Oldbury, Birmingham. He became the mentor I had longed for. He led a thriving church and pioneered Charismatic and healing ministry in the area. Then in 1982 the church released him from leadership so as to enable him and his wife Audrey to move into international ministry. Their wisdom and teaching were in great demand in Italy, Hong Kong, Malaysia, Guyana and Venezuela. They became great friends and over a number of years they taught me so much as we met on courses or visited each other's homes.

Audrey was a registered practitioner of the Myer's Briggs Personality Indicator. When I took the personality test under her guidance, she identified that I was extremely introverted and was able to give me valuable counsel as to how I could grow and thrive in situations that required extroversion such as leading services, preaching and speaking at conferences, taking healing services and dealing with confrontation and failure. I am much indebted to her for her wisdom and guidance in enabling me to understand who I am and what are the appropriate contexts for spiritual growth that my particular personality can resonate with effectively

9

Humble Beginnings

During the time I was receiving this training, I established at Christchurch a monthly healing service produced by the Diocese of Bath and Wells. I had previously looked at several models of public healing ministry and felt most comfortable with the gentle devotional liturgy of the Bath and Wells service. In choosing this liturgy, I was not making any disparaging remarks about the more Pentecostal and Charismatic models, but simply acknowledging that this liturgy most suited my introverted personality and my congregation at the time.

It is always best to start from who you are and where you are, whilst acknowledging that there is always a need to respond to the challenge for personal growth and development. This lesson came to me quite sharply when a vicar who was a friend of mine asked if it would be acceptable to ask people to come forward for prayer during an Evensong service. I told him that he should start with whatever he felt comfortable in his own context. So he advertised that there would be an Evensong service in which the intercessions would be replaced by a time for personal ministry for healing. The parish was buzzing with anticipation. When the service took place there was a bigger congregation than usual. My friend was much encouraged by this and when the time came for the invitation for people to come forward for ministry, the members of the congregation began to look around at each other to see who would go. He said the wait for someone to respond felt like an eternity. In the end an elderly member of the congregation came forward and knelt at the altar rail. Breathing a huge sigh of relief, he asked her what she would like be prayed for. She whispered that she felt sorry for him that he had gone to such lengths to set up the service and that as no one was coming for prayer, she came forward just to support him. He thanked her and prayed a prayer of blessing for her.

No one else came and my friend felt really downhearted. Later that week, he received an emotional phone call from the lady who told him that she had been to the local optician to have a sight test and he confirmed that the sight that she had lost in one eye had been completely restored. My friend hadn't even prayed for her eyesight, but had just asked the Lord to bless her for her faithfulness and love. I guess you can't get more low key than that. But this story just serves to show that healing can happen at the very start of one's venture into the healing ministry.

However, whilst using the healing service of the Diocese of Bath and Wells, I was doing all the praying and got an undesirable reputation of being a 'healer'. So I asked John and Audrey Bedford for advice. They encouraged me to stop praying for people publicly and to train a ministry team. So, over a period of two years I trained a Ministry Team. At the very beginning they were involved in praying in the services and I was quickly able to oversee the ministry time without having much direct involvement. The Lord was so gracious during this time. There were some glorious healings that took place and the ministry team and congregation were greatly blessed at the outcome.

My daughter Sarah was blessed in a somewhat unusual way when she had an accident whilst playing in the vicarage garden with her sister Emma. Sarah pushed the garden swing and the seat came back to hit her full in the face. She came running into the house with blood coming from her mouth. It was a somewhat chaotic scene as Marilyn was busy in the kitchen preparing lunch for a number of guests who were due to arrive at any minute. We sat Sarah in the lounge and tried to stop the bleeding from teeth that were clearly loose. Marilyn shot back into the kitchen as she could smell something burning and I prayed with Sarah that the Lord would bring healing to her mouth and teeth. I told her I would be back in a minute as I was just going to see what was happening in the kitchen. No sooner had I got to the kitchen when Sarah let out a loud cry, so I ran back into the lounge to see Sarah holding a tooth in her hand. I said to her we should now thank Jesus for answering our prayer. After the briefest of prayers, I went back to the kitchen. Once again, no sooner had I got to the kitchen when Sarah let out another loud cry. Running back into the lounge, Sarah was now holding a second tooth. Once again I thanked Jesus for His love and healing and when Sarah had calmed down, I quickly went back to the kitchen. Lo and behold, as soon as I was in the kitchen, Sarah let out a loud cry for the third time. I was expecting Sarah to be holding a third tooth, but she wasn't. Asking her what was the matter, she said, "Dad, can you ask Jesus to stop taking my teeth out." My heart went out to her. I prayed a short prayer and the panic was over. She made a quick recovery and didn't need any hospital or dental treatment.

Some while later, my father brought a colour television to the house as a surprise present. We had never had a colour television and with great excitement I plugged it in and the whole family were amazed at the picture. We never thought we would be able to afford such a luxury and we were still expressing our gratitude when the doorbell rang. On opening the door, there stood a man with a clipboard in hand who proceeded to say he was from the Television Detector Unit and that we did not have a licence for a colour television. I paused for a moment, and then thought that he must be one of Dad's friends and that it was all a windup. So I asked him for his identification, and he pulled from his pocket an identity card with his name on it, 'Steve Morgan'. I laughed and told him he really had me going and I nearly believed him. He protested his name really was Steve Morgan and he wanted to enter the house to see the television. Embarrassment wasn't the word. After profuse apologies, he accepted our story and told us we had 24 hours to get a licence or we would be prosecuted. When he left we all burst into laughter at such an amazing coincidence of plugging in a new television and within five minutes a detector van came past that was driven by a 'Steve Morgan'.

10

Accounts of Healing and Salvation

The following accounts detail something of the breadth of the healing ministry that was unfolding.

The greatest healing of all is to receive the gift of salvation. Joan, who was a faithful member of our church, came to me to say how distressed she was by her husband's attitude to the Christian Faith. Bob was a committed atheist. He had reasoned that there was no God and that those who did believe in God were suffering from a delusion. I had spoken to him on several occasions, and although he was polite, there was no way he wanted anything to do with Christianity. He had a skeptical reply to every attempt at faith sharing and I confess I was at a loss as to what to do. His mind seemed to be completely closed.

Then, one night I had a dream about Bob. He was asleep in bed and Joan was lying beside him in prayer. I had no idea what she was praying but sensed that it was of great significance. I went to see her the following day and told her about the dream. When she asked why I thought it was significant, I was about to tell her that I did not know when all of a sudden I had a mental picture of her holding on to the hem of Bob's pyjamas. I then found myself saying she was to hold the hem of Bob's pyjamas every night and pray that one layer after another of unbelief would be taken away from him until he came to faith. She readily agreed to this and said that she did not have enough faith to believe that he would be converted outright but she did have enough faith to believe that each night the Lord would take away a layer of unbelief.

Weeks went by with no apparent difference in Bob's attitude towards Christianity. Then, one morning he awoke and said to Joan that he believed in God. She did not believe him and told him to shut up because he was just teasing her, and it was in very bad taste. He continued to protest that he now believed in God and Joan continued to tell him off until Bob said that he wanted to go to Church with her. He was true to his word and became one of the most spiritual men in our congregation. As much as he had plumbed the depths of atheism, he now plumbed the depths of the Christian Faith, and the profound insights he received were a source of great encouragement to many people over the ensuing years. Just before Joan passed away, she told me that her whole life had been worthwhile because she had prayed 'The Onion Prayer', as it became known, and lived to see her husband come to faith and receive the greatest gift that a human being can receive, the gift of salvation. Bob continued to be a faithful and prayerful member of the church.

Some while later, Marian came to our church. She had worked with Colin Urquhart at Kingdom Faith, the ministry base we had visited earlier. A match made in heaven was about to unfold. Marian had a wonderful depth of maturity to her faith and this she shared with Bob along with a true servant heart. They shared a great love for the Lord and each other in their marriage. Before the Lord took Bob to Himself, many people visited him and he would pray for them and share what the Lord had been revealing in visions and dreams. We were truly astounded by the glimpses that he had of the afterlife and the insights that he had gleaned from them. Marian made a downstairs bedroom for him and that room emanated such a holy presence it felt like being in a church that had been saturated in prayer for many years. When I visited Bob in his latter days, it was not a case of going to see and pray with someone who was ill, instead it was a privilege to learn from the latest revelations that came from someone who was on his way to glory.

A Muslim lady came to us with a debilitating illness. Her family were wealthy and they had spent a considerable amount of money on visits to specialists over a period of several years. Her condition worsened and she became desperate. She had heard of what was happening at Christchurch and came to one of the services. She said that she was a practising Muslim and asked if she could be prayed for without Jesus being mentioned. This was not a problem. We simply said that we would pray to the One True God. She was extremely happy with that as she felt the use of the words One True God would in no way compromise her religion.

During the prayer time she broke down and sobbed. When asked what was happening, she said she had a picture of Jesus stretching out His hand towards her and felt a strange heat enter her body. We explained that this was quite often experienced by people when they were being healed. We said that we would continue to pray for her and asked her to let us know when the sensation of heat had subsided. A few minutes later she said that the heat had gone. It didn't seem right to invite her to make a connection between her experience and the fact as we used the title One True God it was our belief we were praying to Jesus Christ. So we gave her the invitation to return at any time to let us know the outcome.

A few weeks later she came back and told us that when she got home and told her parents what had happened, they were furious. The dear lady insisted that the only prayer she received was to the One True God and during the time of prayer Jesus appeared to her in a vision. She explained she had not expected this to happen and was extremely surprised when it did. She went on to tell us that the following morning she felt remarkably better, so much so that she contacted her consultant and arranged for a meeting. The consultant ordered a series of tests to be taken and when the results came back he told her she was completely well and would need to be weaned off all of her medication.

After telling her story, she asked what would she have to do to become a Christian. We went through the prayer steps with her and explained that becoming a Christian would be a matter of faith for her in believing every part of the prayers. It seemed such a privilege to spend time with her. She understood and agreed to the prayers that would enable her to become a Christian and leave behind her Muslim faith. She confessed that she had a very enquiring mind and that her Muslim faith had served her well in enabling her to believe in God but she had many questions about her faith that had never adequately been answered. We gave her a taster as it were of the subjects that were dealt with on the *Alpha Course* developed by Rev Nicky Gumbel of Holy Trinity Brompton, London, and which has inspired many thousands of people from all over the world to become Christians. She prayed the prayers and gave her life to Christ and became a Christian, but unfortunately, when she told her family what she had done, they became very aggressive and disowned her. We commended her to a church in Cardiff where they could look after her and give her the nurture and care she needed. After a few years living in Cardiff she moved to England. I lost contact with her for several years until she contacted me to say that she was very happy and was a member of a large Charismatic Anglican church.

11

Deliverance Ministry

My involvement with this ministry only really began after receiving a telephone call from the local newspaper, the *Merthyr Express*. The reporter asked me if I knew that there were five covens in Merthyr Tydfil. I told him that this was the first that I had heard about it. A brief conversation then ensued about what I thought about witchcraft.

The next edition of the *Merthyr Express* had the front page headline, "Vicar of Cyfarthfa discovers five covens in Merthyr". I was horrified as almost immediately I was receiving telephone calls from people asking for help or threatening me with curses. I realised that I was totally unqualified to deal with these issues as I had not had any training whatsoever in my college days.

When I began to research the subject of witchcraft and the demonic, I was amazed at the number of volumes of work written about this subject. The Roman Catholic Church in particular had much to teach in this regard and had great experience to call upon to ensure that a correct diagnosis was made so as to minister successfully in a wide range of contexts such as dealing with witchcraft and witches; breaking curses put on people and places; identifying desecration rituals and restoring those involved in such practices. I found that the services and prayers offered by the Roman Catholic Church were very effective. I discovered that the Protestant Churches had a very varied approach to these subjects but I have to confess that the more I read, the more I became confused and decided that at this stage of my life and ministry I would stick with the insights and ministry that were found in the Roman Catholic Church.

One of the reasons that I did this was because I felt that I was being bombarded with requests for help from members of the public, the Local Authority and the Police. I simply did not have the time to do any in depth research before beginning to respond to the many requests that came my way. I just had to get on with it. The dilemma that I found myself in was how to balance my ministry as a parish priest and at the same time deal with all these requests for help.

What made it even more difficult was that one evening I received a telephone call from someone claiming to belong to a coven in Caerphilly. The person said they were putting a curse on me, knew that my wife Marilyn had recently contracted breast cancer and were praying to their master Satan for her death. When I heard this, I felt shocked and sick to my stomach. I don't think it was righteous indignation when I shouted in anger to the caller that he was worshipping a defeated foe and that Jesus Christ had conquered Satan on the cross. I am afraid the fallen part of my humanity got the better of me after that and I was not proud of myself. I felt absolutely livid that this coven could be so evil as to pray for the destruction of myself and my wife. Following that conversation, I had to be very careful not to go overboard and immerse myself in further research to the detriment of my ministry as a parish priest.

A lady who claimed to be a white witch came for prayer suffering from a chronic back pain. In this instance she was given a private appointment so as to avoid any possible embarrassment, or fear for her, or those around her. She insisted that the powers she had came from God and that witchcraft was a much maligned craft that was indeed perfectly respectable. As a 'white witch', people came to her for healing and she gave several stories of people she had helped. As she told these stories, I took the opportunity of asking the Holy Spirit to lead me as I was not sure what to pray. When she finished I asked her to agree to a prayer being prayed that did not make a judgement call on her practice as a white witch. She was comfortable with this and so I told her the prayer and asked if she could repeat it after me. The prayer went like this. "Jesus, if you are whom you claim to be and if my powers come from God then please make the powers stronger. Jesus, if you are whom you claim to be and if my powers are evil powers then please take them away." She repeated the prayer then fell to the ground and a deep, gruff man's voice came from her, "She belongs to me. You'll never get me out of her." This was the first time that I had heard an evil spirit speak and I have to say I was scared stiff as it was so totally unexpected. Gone was my gentle pastoral voice and I began to forcefully shout prayers of exorcism that I had only read in books. In all honesty, the volume of my voice was more to do with my fear than of a conviction of authority and power.

After about fifteen minutes an unholy noise came from her and she coughed and opened her eyes. As she sat up she asked what had happened. Her back pain had gone, but I felt a constraint in my spirit not to tell her about the spiritual battle that had taken place. This puzzled me at the time, but she contacted me the following week and asked to see me. She told me she had gone back to her spiritualist church, but when she got to the threshold she was overcome with a sense of dread and evil that really frightened her. She could not get in and in fact she didn't want to go in because she felt the place was so evil. I explained to her what had happened when she lay motionless on the floor and that the evil spirit had left her. She was so grateful for not being told beforehand as now she was convinced that spiritualism was an evil enterprise and that the powers that she had were not from God at all but from an evil spirit. She then asked what she had to do to become a Christian and received prayers of healing through repentance.

A Christian psychiatrist contacted me about a very distressing case that left him completely baffled. A seven year old boy had been referred to him whose behaviour had become bizarre following a Ouija board session with friends. This normally well behaved boy had become disruptive in school and at home. He was making animal noises and hissing like a snake at anyone who confronted him about his behaviour. Then, one day, he took a hammer to the family tortoise and was discovered eating the flesh. The poor parents were absolutely horrified and were very quickly referred to a psychiatrist.

After a period of time interviewing and monitoring the boy, the psychiatrist became convinced the boy was possessed by an evil spirit and needed exorcism. Working alongside the psychiatrist, an exorcism was performed and the young lad made a complete recovery. This was not the first time I had been asked by a psychiatrist to perform an exorcism, but it was the first time it was actually necessary to perform such a service. On previous occasions, I was able to offer a diagnosis that did not necessitate an exorcism. Afterwards, the boy was monitored for a while whilst being gradually taken off his medication and then discharged from care. He made a complete recovery and mercifully had little memory of the months when he was so unwell.

One day a very distressed husband came to me to ask me to exorcise his wife. He said that she was hearing a voice that told her to do things that made him fearful for his life. Apparently, she would behave quite normally for weeks at a time and then suddenly change and begin to throw things at him. She was a loving wife and was distressed by what was happening. She said she seemed to lose all control and hearing a voice that told her to kill him as he was evil. She went on to explain that she heard the voice most days but she was able to resist it until it grew so loud and aggressive that she lost all will power to resist and then she actually wanted to do what it was telling her. She had readily agreed to receive treatment and was diagnosed with the functional psychosis of schizophrenia. However, the medication wasn't producing the desired result and so they were looking for any alternative that might help. At this point I would like to say that the performing of an exorcism is usually the last resort and only carried out after all other avenues have been exhausted. In this instance, she didn't have any significant stress or deprivation factors that are often associated with the illness and so I encouraged her to go on a diet that had no refined flour in it. I remembered reading a book a few months earlier which detailed research findings that identified the consumption of refined white flour as the culprit able to set up an allergic reaction in the brain and produce the functional psychosis symptom of hearing voices. A significant number of patients were relieved of all symptoms by being placed on this diet.

Her poor husband was not at all impressed by this suggestion and I could tell by his face that he thought I had 'bottled it' and that I was fobbing them off. Seeing this, I went on to explain the importance of correct diagnosis. If I was to perform an exorcism and there was no evil spirit present that could account for her condition then they would be left in a very confused and unhealthy state of mind. I gave them an illustration of a person who was brought to me after having gone to a number of 'exorcists' to no avail. They were relentless in their quest to find an exorcist who was powerful enough to deal with their situation. I told them a small number of people believing themselves to be possessed had been completely healed as a result of going on a diet that did not contain refined white flour. The poor lady protested to her partner that she was exhausted and frustrated by being taken to a string of exorcists and could she please be allowed to at least try the diet. The partner reluctantly agreed and asked if I would be willing to speak to her psychiatrist and tell him about the diet. He saw no problem with her going on this diet as it would not conflict with the medication he was prescribing. It must have been at least nine months later that I had a telephone call to say that she was now well again and very grateful.

On hearing this story, the couple seemed to relax and agreed that going on the diet could at least do no harm. The husband then asked me if I would do an exorcism if the diet didn't work. I evaded the question because there were other avenues that would need to be explored before an exorcism became necessary. In this instance, the couple gave me regular updates of the continued improvement in the condition and about six months later they gave me the great news that the psychiatrist had discharged her and that she was now no longer taking any medication. A year later they let me know that all was well and that there was no reoccurrence of the condition.

In 1985, Alison and her husband John attended one of the healing services and she came to the altar rail for ministry. I asked her what I should pray for. She explained that she was unable to have children and that she was scheduled to meet with a consultant at the hospital with a view to having an operation as a possible cure for her condition. As I prayed for her, I felt a great sense that the Lord was healing her right there and then. A prophetic word came to me and I was about to share it with Alison when I had a check in my spirit so I did not speak it out. As the couple were leaving the church I sensed a release in my spirit to speak out the prophetic word. However, the word was so specific that I was quite nervous in delivering it. All sorts of doubts came crashing into my mind as I spoke out the prophetic word. If I had not heard the Lord correctly then I would be in serious trouble and would cause great distress to the couple. I said to John that the Lord had healed his wife and that she would be giving birth to a daughter before Christmas that year. Not long afterwards, Alison became pregnant and I baptised their baby daughter on the Sunday before Christmas. They appropriately named their baby, Faith. Faith gave birth to Faith.

I have found that when I minister a prophetic Word or a Word of knowledge for someone, I very rarely receive the Word firstly in my mind and then speak it out. I invariably sense the presence of the Holy Spirit in my spirit and simply speak out the Word. My spirit is quickened by the Holy Spirit and I find myself speaking with a level of assuredness that is beyond what I receive when I am teaching or preaching. There may be many reasons for this, but I take the view that, on most occasions when I find myself speaking a prophetic Word or a Word of knowledge, if I knew what it was beforehand then I might not have enough courage to speak it out at a later moment.

This was starkly illustrated when a lady came forward for prayer at a Church Healing Service. I asked her what she wanted the Lord to do for her and she said that she wanted to be healed of her arthritis. Taking hold of her arthritic hands, I was about to pray when I prophesied that if she gave up the adulterous relationship she was in, then the Lord would bless her and heal her. If I had received those words in my mind before speaking, then I honestly do not believe that I would have had the courage to have spoken them out. I felt certain that if it had not been for the quickening of my spirit by the Holy Spirit, then there is no way that those words would ever have come out of my mouth.

The lady looked up at me and said nobody knew of her secret liaison. I told her that was not true because the Lord knew. She sobbed and asked God to forgive her and to give her the strength to end the immoral relationship. I saw her many months later and she told me she had confessed the relationship to her husband and he had forgiven her. She then ended the immoral relationship and when she showed me her hands, the fingers were almost straight again and the swollen knuckles had subsided. It is easy to sing or pray about the omnipresence of God, but it is at moments like these that I realise the practical reality of that truth. Our Lord and God sees and hears everything we do and say. There are no secret places where He cannot see or hear. He sees our every act and hears our every word and even our thoughts. The most astounding thing is that in spite of all the knowledge that He has about us, He still loves us and encourages us with forgiveness and healing so we may experience our real heart's desire – to see Him glorified in and through our lives.

An exception to my usual experience of not receiving a Word of knowledge outside of a ministry situation took place one day when I was cleaning the rubbish that had blown into the vicarage garden. I picked up a receipt from our local B&Q store and noticed that it had been signed by a former church member. Joan had left the church because at that time we did not have anyone to lead our young people and she was concerned about her daughter's spiritual development. As I looked at the receipt, I sensed the Lord speaking to me as I heard the words, "Tell Joan it's time to come home". I immediately went back into the vicarage and telephoned Joan. She was ecstatic as she had just had a time of prayer and had asked the Lord to confirm His prompting by me telephoning her with the words, "It's time to come home". Joan, her husband Peter and daughter Kathryn were welcomed back with open arms. Kathryn went on to Bible College and Joan and Peter proved to be a great blessing.

The husband of one of our members was sent to prison for an offence whilst working for a national bank. During that time, the church supported her and her children as she found it impossible to manage without her husband's salary. It was a time in which we were blessed as a church for the privilege of being able to show the family how much we loved and cared for them.

When David was released from prison, he came to church the very next Sunday. He said to me after the service that he had come to thank me and the church for all that had been done to support his family during the time he was in prison. He went on to say that he would not attend church again as he did not believe in God. As he was telling me this, I suddenly felt the presence of the Holy Spirit. It was as if I was listening to myself as the words came out. I asked him what the chances were of him getting a job. He replied that having just got out of prison, there was no chance. My voice had changed in tone, and I was now speaking with an assuredness that was way beyond the natural. I told him that God wanted him and that he could set the day when he would return to work. David looked at me as if I had two heads. He took up the challenge, not believing for a moment that anything would happen, and said he would like to start work in two weeks time. Then I said to him that God wanted him to be absolutely certain that it was He who would provide the job, so he would start in two weeks time on the Monday of that week. To be absolutely sure that God would provide this, I told him that it would be a job involving responsibility for money, and there would be a number of applicants who would be more qualified than he was and who did not have criminal records. David replied that if that happened then he would become a Christian and come with his wife to church. I can honestly say that my response to what I had spoken to David was one of high elation and utter certainty that the Lord would do this, such was the sense of the presence and ministry of the Holy

Spirit at the time. Sure enough, David began his new job on the Monday, and there were eleven other candidates who had applied for the job, none of whom had criminal records. David was true to his word. He became a Christian and came to church with his wife. His Christian growth was prodigious and it wasn't very long before he became a member of our leadership team.

One of our church members was extremely devout. She was married to Des, a very pleasant man who claimed to be a complete atheist. When I visited his wife, Norma, we would have quite deliberate conversations about the Christian faith so that Des would hear and perhaps respond. Although he overheard a number of our conversations, he never responded and seemed quite uninterested. Then, one day, Des became ill and was admitted to the Intensive Care Unit of the local hospital. The family were summoned to the hospital to say their farewells as he was in a coma and close to death. I asked if I could see him alone. Sitting at his bedside, I took his hand and spoke to him as if he was conscious, being aware that on some occasions comatose patients were able to recall conversations in their presence. I told him that I was going to tell him in a few sentences what was the message of Jesus to the world. When I had finished, I asked him to squeeze my hand if he had heard me and had decided to give his life to Jesus Christ. He squeezed my hand. I then said that I needed to be absolutely sure that he had heard me and made the decision to accept Jesus Christ into his life as Lord and Saviour by squeezing my hand twice. He did this with firm grips each time and immediately afterwards, the heart monitor flatlined and he died. I never cease to be amazed at how patient and merciful the Lord is in His dealings with humankind. He never gives up on anybody and as long as there is breath in a person, there is always hope.

On another occasion, I was asked by a family to pray for a lady who was close to the point of death. She was connected to a variety of medical machines. Shortly after I prayed and anointed her, there was a sound of feet rushing down the corridor. Several medical personnel burst through the door and entered her room. They told me to stay in the corner and not to move whilst they hurriedly disconnected her from some of the machines and re-attached her to new ones. Apparently the alarms had gone off at the Nursing Station indicating that there was something wrong. When the replacement machines were successfully connected, the doctor said he had no explanation of what had happened. All the machines now indicated that she was perfectly healthy. I just sat on the chair in the corner awestruck by what had happened. The lady concerned was discharged from hospital shortly afterwards.

Some while later, I made an appointment with Bishop Roy Davies to inform him of what had been happening in the parish, and to discuss our plans for its future development. I arrived a little early and as I was waiting in his office, his secretary told me that the Bishop had some bad news and that he needed an operation on his spine which would result in him having to resign.

After a few minutes, the Bishop entered the office, walking rather gingerly. His secretary told him she had let me know the news of his impending operation. I offered to pray for him right there and then. I prayed with thanksgiving for the life of faith and ministry of the Bishop and then asked the Lord to reveal His love for the Bishop by healing his spine. The Bishop fell to the floor immediately and Betty, his horrified secretary, waggled her wrists back and fore whilst hopping from one leg to the other and cried to me, "What have you done to the Bishop?" I explained that sometimes people fall to the floor when they are physically overcome by the presence and power of the Lord. The secretary became even more agitated, and asked what we should do. I told her that we needed to leave him there whilst he was being ministered to by the Lord. He was only on the floor for a few minutes, but it seemed like an age. When the Bishop got to his feet, he said that he had no pain in his spine, and I advised him to have another medical checkup as he had probably been healed. The Bishop then told me something that really saddened me. He said I was the first priest in his ministry ever to offer personal prayer. He did go for a medical checkup and had the good news that his spine no longer needed an operation and he could look forward to continuing his ministry as our Bishop.

12

House Blessings

Another consequence of the *Merthyr Express* publishing the false claim that I had discovered five covens in Merthyr Tydfil was that I had a stream of requests to deal with alleged hauntings in the area. I had only done cursory reading on the topic as none of this was dealt with when I was in college. Why oh why was there no teaching on this subject when I was training to be a priest? It was like sending out an AA patrolman without such things as spanners and screwdrivers. I was totally ill-equipped for these challenges and so I had to cram in as much knowledge as possible in a very short period of time. It was a steep learning curve for me and my Church.

One of the first requests came from the Local Authority. I was asked to visit a block of flats where a number of the residents had complained about apparitions and objects being moved or broken. When we got to the first flat, the lady told us of several incidents that had frightened her. A window had been smashed from the inside whilst she was sitting on the settee; a sword that was hanging on a wall, suddenly shot across the room; strange handprints would appear going up a wall and across the ceiling. My first instinct was to put it all down to a vivid and overactive imagination. Perhaps she was making it all up because she just wanted to be moved into another flat. Perhaps she was lonely and just wanted attention. I confess that I didn't have a clue as to how to evaluate her story. I was a complete novice and didn't I know it. This was brought sharply into focus when I noticed that a handprint started to appear on the wall behind the lady, then another one just above the first one. My heart began to race and all I wanted to do was to get out of there as fast as I could. But I was the Vicar, and I was supposed to know what to do. The truth is that I didn't have the first clue, so we prayed several prayers, and then I said that I needed to do further research, and I would return as soon as possible. When I eventually returned, the matter was resolved and there were no further such experiences. The reason for this is what we found in a second flat.

Alan, one of our Church members who was with me, and I ascended a flight of stairs, at one point on the stairs, the temperature dropped markedly. It was so cold that we could see our breath over a span of four stairs. My reading on the subject thus far enabled me to identify this area as the setting in which someone had died in a highly charged emotional context. We prayed the appropriate prayers and the temperature returned to normal.

When I contacted the Local Authority afterwards, I was informed that a person had committed suicide by hanging himself from the banisters. It was when we got to the landing that I saw my first ghost. It was quite amusing actually. Alan had the bowl of Holy Water, and as we faced each other on the landing he suddenly froze. I asked him what was wrong. He was slowly raising the bowl of Holy Water and said he was going to pour the Holy Water all over his head and then he was going to leg it out of there as fast as God gave him the strength. I asked him again what was the matter. With the stiff lips of a ventriloquist he mumbled the words, "Have you seen what's behind you?" Turning around quickly, I looked down a passageway and facing us was a small bathroom. The door was open, and there it was, an image of a nude lady sitting on the toilet. I took the bowl of Holy Water from Alan and went towards the image. Whilst praying the appropriate prayers I thrust my hand into the Holy Water and sprayed the apparition. There was a hissing sound, and the ghost disappeared. Interestingly, the water seemed to disappear or evaporate and there was no trace of it in the toilet area. It was fortunate that I had done some research on ghosts and although there is a lot of Hollywood imagination in the literature on the subject, there is nevertheless a corpus of literature that is well researched. I discovered that the technical name for a ghost is a 'Place Memory'. Apparently, when there is a considerable discharge of human emotion, the very fabric of the physical environment can act as a kind of video recorder, and under certain conditions, a kind of playback can take place in which the 'Place Memory' can be seen and/or heard. It is also possible to pick up a distinct smell or feeling. The feeling sensation is not that of physical touch but of a change in temperature or a kind of foreboding.

One Sunday evening, I was taking a Confirmation class in the Church hall, when two policemen rushed in and asked if I was the vicar of Cyfarthfa. When I replied in the affirmative, they ordered me to go with them. We were all taken aback and the class thought I was being arrested. When I asked the officers what was the matter, they replied that they needed to take me to a house in a nearby village as there was a house disturbance. Whilst in the police car, the officers explained that a neighbour had telephoned the police to say there was an hysterical woman running down the street shouting out that there was something in her house. When the officers arrived at the house, they were told there was someone in an upstairs bedroom making a dreadful noise. They entered the house and made their way up the stairs. They heard a noise coming from a bedroom and went in to see what it was. There was nobody to be seen, but when the blood-curdling noise was suddenly heard, they fled out of the house.

We parked outside the house and I foolishly asked the officers if they would lead me to the bedroom where the noise had been heard. I can't repeat what they said, but with the use of very colourful language they declined the request. As I went up the stairs, I could hear a noise that sounded like someone desperately gasping for breath. Once again, as I prayed in the room and sprayed Holy Water into the four corners, the water evaporated before it touched the wall and the noise stopped. I found out later that a previous occupant of the house had died in that bedroom.

The man had emphysema and his oxygen cylinder had run out. The awful sounds that were heard were the last desperate breaths of the poor man.

Melanie, a *BBC Wales* reporter, asked me if it would be possible for her to be with me when I conducted a service to deal with a 'Place Memory'. I said that she could accompany me if it was just a 'Place Memory' that had to be dealt with as 'Place Memories' were not evil in themselves, even though they are often portrayed as such.

Some while later I received a telephone call from a distressed lady in Dowlais, which is an area of Merthyr Tydfil. What she described to me seemed a perfect fit for Melanie's request. Having received all the necessary permissions, it was agreed that the 'Place Memory' would be dealt with live during a *BBC Wales* programme that was hosted by Vincent Kane. Melanie and I interviewed the lady in her lounge and she told us a man would appear on the top of her stairs with a fierce look on his face. Before the man would appear there would be a knocking noise that gradually increased in volume.

Vincent explained to his listeners what was taking place. He then said there would be a pause whilst the lady, Melanie and myself went to the top of the stairs to conduct the service. When we came back on air, we were asked to explain to the listeners what was happening. As Vincent was talking to Melanie, live on air, Melanie suddenly interjected and told Vincent to be quiet. Vincent was taken aback by this and asked what was the matter. Melanie explained that her recording equipment was detecting a slight sound when no one was talking, so she insisted that Vincent be quiet for a few moments. Melanie whispered that the recording dial was moving higher and higher. Then, all of a sudden, there was an audible knocking noise. At this point, Melanie lost all composure and shouted, "Oh s…!" She dropped all her equipment and ran into a nearby bathroom, slamming the door behind her whilst shouting that she was not going to come out until whatever it was had been dealt with!

Although poor Melanie was terrorised by the whole event, it was all recorded on her equipment. She later told me that at the *BBC Wales* Christmas party they would play some of the funniest news stories and mistakes of the year. Much to her chagrin, her recording at Dowlais became a highlight of the party. In spite of Melanie's unforeseen histrionics, the Place Memory was successfully dealt with.

Not long after this incident, I had a telephone call from the producers of the *Esther Rantzen Show*. They wanted me to appear on a programme that was going to deal with the issue of ghosts. I thought that this might be a good opportunity of allaying people's fears and misunderstandings and so accepted the invitation. It was an all-expenses paid trip to London and an overnight stay in a very nice hotel. I was picked up at the train station and driven to the studio for the afternoon rehearsal.

About a hundred people from various walks of life had been invited. The producers asked those assembled a number of questions regarding their personal experiences and beliefs. I had not realised that after the rehearsal they would pick five people from amongst those who had been invited to be on the main stage with Esther. I was chosen to be on stage and one of the producers then ushered me towards the make-up room. I sat down and the make-up lady said I would be a challenging client. Apparently, I had the kind of head that was best suited for radio. I thought she was trying to get on my good side, until I realised she was serious!

After the facial scrubs, she then put some kind of undercoat on my bald patch before painting it and powdering it so there would be no glare. Then she did the same to my face with different coloured powders. However, the coup de grace came when she opened a large cupboard containing a vast array of lipsticks. This was the last straw. I was already feeling like a clown being prepared for the circus. She knew she had met her nemesis when I told her in no uncertain terms, "Listen here, lovely girl. I come from Merthyr Tydfil. If you put that colour on these lips, I will become the laughing stock of the town and I will never live it down." She tried to gently persuade me to change my mind but this man was not for turning. Following a loud exhalation of breath, she retorted that she would have to start all over again. Keeping my lips a neutral colour, she then blended a new set of pastes and potions to match. Little did I know at the time that as well as preparing me for the show, she had also taken her revenge.

The show got really heated and there were some quite bizarre contributions being made. Just as Esther was beginning to lose control of the proceedings, a producer frantically motioned to her to ask me to speak. As soon as I had finished, it was announced they had finished the recording. The producer thanked me for my contribution and I told him that at least I hadn't make a spectacle of myself. He laughed, but very shortly afterwards, the make-up girl would have laughed even louder. Back at the hotel, I went straight into the shower. When I had finished, I grabbed a lovely clean white bath towel and began drying my face. Guess what? The towel was full of make-up. I looked in the mirror and saw what looked like the best man at Count Dracula's wedding. My head was covered with congealed streaks of colour as all the layers mixed together to leave me looking like a character in a horror movie. Back in the shower I went and frantically washed and washed. Getting out, I grabbed the second bath towel and dried my face. Guess what? The towel was full of make-up again. I think the make-up girl must have used glue. The next time I stood in front of the bathroom mirror and used a nail brush and soap. The make-up did eventually come off, but I ended up looking like a lobster.

In the morning I went to the reception desk to apologise and explain why the towels in my room were in such a state. Before I could say anything, the receptionist asked if I was feeling well because my face was so red. When I told her what had happened she ruined her own make-up whilst blotting the tears from her eyes as she tried, unsuccessfully, to retain any semblance of professional composure.

13

Jesus Died to Destroy Death – an Understanding at Last

For Christians, the ultimate healing is what happens after death, when we take on a perfectly healthy resurrection body in heaven. My understanding of what happens at death was transformed by three incidents that happened in a fairly short period of time.

I had been puzzled for a number of years by two extracts from the Gospel of John which are in the Anglican Order of Service for the Burial of the Dead. The first extract is from John 11:25-26,

> *"I am the resurrection and the life; says the Lord; he who believes in me, though he die, yet shall he live; and whoever lives and believes in me shall never die."*

These verses convey clearly the obvious assertion that Christian believers will pass from this life to the afterlife. However, I was intrigued by the last phrase which states *'whoever lives and believes in me shall never die'*. Surely, we all have to die, so in what sense can it be said that Christian believers never die?

I had read a number of Bible commentaries but was never really satisfied with their explanations of these verses. I felt the same sense of dissatisfaction when reading commentaries on John 14:1-3,

> *"Let not your hearts be troubled; you believe in God, believe also in me. In my Father's house are many dwelling places, if it were not so, would I have told you*

*that I go to prepare a place for you? And when I go
and prepare a place for you, I will come again and will
take you to myself, that where I am you may be also."*

In these verses, I was puzzled by the reference that Jesus will
come again and take us to Himself. In what sense does Jesus come
to us when we are dying and then take us to Himself? I wondered
if these verses contained more than propositional truths
concerning Christian believers' relationship with Jesus and going
to heaven.

The first incident took place on Christmas Day 1984. Marie's
mother, Vi, had been ill for some while and for several days she
had been in a coma. On Christmas Day a doctor was summoned
to the house. Members of the family were gathered and were
sitting around the bed. Suddenly Vi turned to her husband, Bryn,
who was sitting at the foot of the bed and asked him to stand up
and move to one side so she was able to see Jesus who was
standing behind him. Bryn and those gathered at the bedside were
understandably stunned by this request. Eventually, Bryn moved
to one side and then Vi raised her hands and said, "I'm ready. I'm
coming now". A short while afterwards, Vi ceased to breathe.

The second incident also took place at a Christmastime.
Norma's family telephoned to ask me to come to her house as they
knew she was close to death. When I got there, Norma was in bed
and very weak. It appeared as if she was sleeping so I prayed in a
gentle whisper. Norma opened her eyes and after a few moments
she said, "Look Steve. It's Jesus, and He's standing right behind
you." I turned around quickly but didn't see anyone. When I said
to Norma that I could't see anyone she retorted with typical
candour, "Oh, you dup, never mind". With that, she raised her
hands towards Jesus, on whom she was focusing, and began to
express her faith. Then she stopped in mid-sentence and said,
"Pardon. (Pause) Can you say that again? (Pause) Oh, yes please".
With that her arms flopped down onto the bed and they were the
last words she uttered. She remained breathing for some
considerable while afterwards before she died.

Now, if her last words bore testimony that Jesus Himself came for her, then that witnesses to the words of Jesus, *"I will come and take you to myself"*. Moreover, if the Lord took her to Himself at that time, then her physical body continued to breathe for a while afterwards. This would make sense of the Lord's words, *"...Whoever lives and believes in me shall never die"*. Does this mean that whoever lives and believes in Jesus as Lord and Saviour will never experience what it is like to die? If Norma was taken by Jesus a little while before her physical body ceased to breathe, then she would not have had the experience of dying because she was not there when it happened.

The third incident made up my mind once and for all. I was visiting a parishioner at the local hospital when I happened to pass a patient in a single bed unit. I recognised her to be Gwyneth, a Nursing Sister, who I had met a number of times when she was nursing in the Post-Natal department. There had been several occasions when I had been called to the hospital in my capacity as one of the hospital chaplains to minister to distressed parents and relatives in their concern for their children. I held Gwyneth in the highest regard. She was just a fabulous human being, a real gift to distressed and grieving parents. Her gentle manner and empathy were hugely appreciated, and she always took time to answer their questions and reassure them that everything possible was being done for their children. On the occasions when babies died, she would weep with the parents and hold the mothers with such a loving care. Having said all that about Gwyneth, there was one thing that she lacked. She did not have a faith and confessed to me privately that what she witnessed in her professional life had caused her to lose all faith in God. Having seen her, now as a patient, in the single bed unit, I turned and entered her room. Before I could say anything, she said to me that she knew why I had come and that I could go away because she was not interested. I explained I was on my way to visit a parishioner on her ward and had not made a special journey to see her. Her uncharacteristic aggression died down and I sat at her bedside as she explained that she only had a short time to live. While she told me her story, I prayed in my mind for the Lord to please give me something to say that was meaningful to her.

The thought that such a wonderful human being would not be going to heaven was so obnoxious to me that I was hardly listening to what she had to say as I pleaded with the Lord do something or give me something to say. I then found myself asking her if there was anything that she was frightened of. She said that there was. When she woke up in the morning, her cancerous lungs were so full of fluid that she had the sensation of drowning. She would press the panic button and the staff would then undertake a procedure to relieve the situation. She told me she had always been afraid of drowning and her experience every morning was a living nightmare for her. I now sensed the presence of the Holy Spirit and a surge of faith. I asked her if I could visit her before she woke up and told her I would sit in the corner of the room and pray silently in my mind, not out loud, for the Lord to come and do something for her to relieve her from her panic. She said she was so frightened that she would say 'Yes' to anything. So I asked her what time she woke up in the mornings and she said it was about 4.30am. My heart sank. What had I let myself in for? I had never been the best at getting up early in the morning, but 4.30am was just ridiculous. I set the alarm for 3.30am so I could be at her bedside by 4am.

When I arrived, I sat in a chair in the corner and prayed that the Lord would do whatever He could for her so she would get to heaven. I did not pray for her healing, but found myself pleading for her salvation. When she woke up, there was no fluid in her lungs. The look of surprise and relief in her eyes was a delight to behold. However, disappointingly, she did not put this down to my prayers, but instead she said perhaps she was getting better. I was not daunted by this, and asked if I could come the following morning and do the same things – sit in the chair and pray that the Lord would come and help her. She agreed and I duly arrived at 4am the following morning. Again, she awoke and there was no fluid in her lungs. She told me she had asked her doctor the previous day what might account for her not having any fluid in her lungs when she woke up. She wondered if she was getting better. He told her he was bemused by her experience and that her condition was not improving. In fact, with great frankness, he told her she was in the last stage of her illness. Once more, Gwyneth did not make any connection between my presence and prayers and the fact that she did not wake up with fluid in her lungs. She simply asked if I could come again on the following morning.

When she woke up on this third morning with no fluid in her lungs she had begun to make the connection I was pleading for. She said that if I came once more, the following morning, she would ask me what she would have to do to become a Christian. I was absolutely overjoyed and had a great sense of anticipation for the next morning. Sure enough, she awoke with no fluid in her lungs and I was able to go through the prayers needed so she could confess her sins, make a declaration of faith, and invite Jesus into her life to be her Lord and Saviour. It was such an outstanding privilege to be with her for those life-changing moments. I then said I would like to come to the hospital every morning at the same time, until Jesus came to take her to Himself. When I arrived the following morning, the Sister told me that Gwyneth had slipped into a coma and she only had a short time left. I asked her for permission to sit at the bedside so I could pray for her and read some Psalms to her, explaining that sometimes patients in a coma are able to hear what is going on around them. The Sister readily agreed and I sat on a chair at the bedside praying with thanksgiving that Gwyneth now belonged to Jesus and would be receiving all of His promises of heaven and a perfectly restored resurrection body.

What happened next is something that completely took my breath away. As God is my witness, she began to sing, and this is what she sang.

> "Oh God our help in ages past,
> Our hope for years to come,
> Our shelter from the stormy blast,
> And our eternal home."

She was still in the coma. She sang the same words again and then squeezed my hand as if to indicate that I should sing with her. I joined her, and we both sang the words again as it was from a well know hymn. Then we sang it again. At that moment the door opened and the Sister and a doctor stood in the doorway looking at a patient in a coma and a priest singing a duet. They walked silently backwards and slowly closed the door. Meanwhile Gwyneth and I continued to sing the same verse over and over again. Then she took her hand from mine, raised her hands, looked at the corner of the room and said, "Jesus, you've come. I'm so, so sorry it's taken me such a long time to believe in you." She was partly through another sentence when she paused and said, "I'm sorry, can you say that again? (Pause) Do you mean now? (Pause) Oh yes please." With that her arms fell down and a few days later her earthly body stopped breathing.

I am longing to meet with people such as Gwyneth again, but I do believe that by the time my earthly body ceases to breathe, I will not be there. I will be gone because the Lord will have fulfilled His promise to take me to Himself and to do so before death. Truly He has conquered death that we might not have to experience death.

14

Time for a Marathon

On the Sunday afternoon of March 29th 1981, I watched the highlights of the first London Marathon on the television. I was captivated by the event and the carnival atmosphere as runners of all abilities, shapes and sizes took part. Before the Sunday evening service, I mentioned to the choir that I would love to take part in such an event. The reply quickly came back that I was past it and it could only be a pipe dream. Past it? How dare they? In the next few minutes I challenged them all to come to the vicarage the following evening and we would start to train for a Marathon.

News got around and a dozen men arrived at my door to begin the challenge. It was hilarious. We all started off at a gallop down the steep hill and on towards the Leisure Centre at Rhydycar which was less than a mile away. Before we got to Rhydycar, we were all euphemistically quite unwell. In fact it would be more accurate to say we thought we were dying. Gasping for breath and hardly able to speak, we realised the stupidity of trying to look good in front of each other whilst ignoring the fact that we were hopelessly unfit. It was a good lesson to learn and one which provided a great sermon illustration the following Sunday.

One by one, the members of the group started to fall away until there were only two of us left. Peter and I trained for six months to be able to run the Cardiff Marathon on September 26th. When we arrived at the starting line, it seemed the competitors were divided into three groups; the 'well prepared', the 'well well well', and the 'well meaning'. The 'well prepared' were the athletes taking part; the 'well well well' were the 'let's have a go brigade' that were made up of a variety of laughing specimens from the emaciated to the obese. The 'well meaning' included Peter and myself.

One of the 'well prepared' looked at what Peter and I had on our feet and politely asked if we had forgotten to put on our running shoes. We were wearing solid soled football trainers and had done all our training in them. When we confessed that our well-worn trainers were all that we had, he put the wind up us by saying we would never be able to run a full marathon in them.

The starter's gun fired and the 4000 competitors set off from Cardiff Castle. We began the race at a leisurely ten minutes a mile pace and had only gone about three miles when the runners in the 'well well well' group started to fall by the wayside, and fall they did. They were exhausted already, and sat on the kerbs waiting to be picked up.

The race started in fine weather but by the time we got to the seven mile marker the heavens opened and a hail storm saw runners sheltering in telephone boxes and by the side of cars and hedges. At the eleven mile mark in Barry, the weather improved and the sun came out, but at eighteen miles, in Penarth, the heavens opened again and we found ourselves having to run through a few inches of water for a couple of miles. Such was the deluge that even the spectators on the pavements were standing in water. At the end of the race, there was glorious sunshine and Peter and I had finished in four hours and twenty minutes. We had confounded the doubters and had blistered feet to prove it.

After the Cardiff Marathon, I continued to run, and found the released endorphins were a great help in coping with the stresses and strains of life issues. I needed to set myself a goal in order to keep up the enthusiasm and so decided I wanted to run a marathon in under four hours. This was not accomplished until I ran in the London Marathon in 1992. On this occasion, John was my running partner. However, when we got to the six mile mark, where the Cutty Sark was berthed, John became very fatigued and told me to carry on without him or I would never beat the four hour mark. When I reached the eighteen mile marker there were loud cheers from the crowd for runners who were about a hundred yards ahead of me. I decided to catch them up and to my surprise it was a group led by the famous Steve Cram. The feeling of elation that I had when I overtook him was overwhelming. As well as beating the four hour barrier, I had also beaten Steve Cram. Meanwhile, back in Merthyr Tydfil, one of our members was penning this little ditty.

Our Vicar (The Marathon Man)

What a wonderful chap is our vicar.
A man in a race against time.
He's up like a lark in the morning,
And welcomes each day with a smile.

After gulping a handful of ginseng,
It's on with his shorts and his vest,
Then he's off down the hill like a bullet
Determined to give of his best.

The marathon looms ever nearer.
Will his training pay off in the end?
Will his legs start to wobble like jelly?
On his stamina can he depend?

His masculine chest is a problem.
The hairs tangled up in his vest,
So he shaves them off with his razor
And is ready to run with the best.

"I'll finish the race if it kills me.
I'll drag myself over that line."
Determined and plucky as ever,
He arrives at the start just in time!

Back at the church we're all waiting.
Anxiously waiting for news.
Will the vicar arrive on a stretcher?

We patiently sit in our pews.
In comes the vicar triumphant.
His face is aglow with delight.
Without speaking, we all knew he made it.
"Well done lad, we're wrong! You were right!"

To his sermons we've listened each Sunday.
He's certainly helped put us right.
As a sheepdog, he's one in a million,
Though his bark is much worse than his bite.

Let's all drink a toast to our vicar,
Our counsellor, pastor and friend.
He's served each one without question.
On his loyalty we can depend.

But don't envy the task of a vicar
And think that he hasn't a care.
Just give him the warm hand of friendship
And remember your vicar in prayer.

15

John Wimber Comes to London

In 1984 I attended a conference at Westminster Central Hall in London led by John Wimber and his team from the Vineyard Church at Anaheim, California. What I heard, and what I saw, astounded me and I was reduced to tears on numerous occasions. At the very first session, as we were worshipping, a man called out that the Lord wanted to heal the blind who were there. John Wimber swiftly replied that he had not 'heard' the Lord telling him that the Lord wanted to heal the blind, and so we were directed to continue in worship. When the worship concluded John Wimber began to teach and then paused for a moment. He then said the man was right and the Lord did want to heal blind people at the meeting. He went on to say he felt the Lord did not want him to pray personally for any blind people who were there but that the delegates were to turn and pray for the nearest blind person to them. I felt disappointed and a wave of doubt came over me concerning John Wimber's ministry. I thought it was a bit of a cop out on his part so if no one was healed we would get the blame and not him.

We were requested to stay where we were, identify the nearest blind person and ask them if they wanted prayer. Without any further instruction, we were asked to pray for those individuals. As I looked to my right, there was a man about eight seats away in the row below me who had a Guide Dog. Such was the poverty of my faith in that moment that I slowly looked to my left, in front of me and behind me, to see if there was someone nearer who was blind. In all truth, it was the sight of the Guide Dog that left me confused and lacking in faith for his healing. Very quickly, people began to huddle together as they drew closer to the blind man. I joined them somewhat half-heartedly and began to pray. I remember saying to the Lord that I really wanted to believe and asked Him to help me in my state of unbelief. A few minutes later the blind man began to cry and shortly afterwards those praying for him were told the reason he was crying was because he could now see and he was afraid he would have his faithful Guide Dog taken from him. I was speechless as I was humbled. Slumped back in my seat, I pleaded with the Lord to give me the faith to truly believe for healing in the face of human impossibilities.

Several blind people claimed they had been healed, but John Wimber said he was not prepared to accept anyone's word for it unless they were able to bring back medical verification that they had actually been blind and could now see. He added that his caution was based on experiences of some people in America who attended services with a white stick and wearing dark glasses whilst claiming to be blind. Then they would go forward for prayer and claim falsely to be healed. They misguidedly thought they were doing God a favour, but in fact they were bringing the ministry of healing into disrepute. One person did return to the Conference armed with his medical records as proof that he had been registered as blind when he attended the first day of the Conference and that his vision had been totally restored. Apparently his blindness was a consequence of being diabetic. I never saw the man with the Guide Dog again and often wonder what happened to them.

By the time that the conference was drawing to a close, the meetings were being relayed to several churches nearby to accommodate the many hundreds of people who wanted to hear the teaching and see the Lord healing many individuals. One evening, as I was walking along the Thames Embankment to the meeting at Westminster Central Hall from the flat where I was staying, I found myself catching up someone whom I presumed to be homeless. He was very dishevelled and wore a large overcoat tied with string. On his feet seemed to be improvised shoes also tied with string. As I approached him, I knew that I should have stopped but I would have been late for the meeting so I carried on walking. Although I upbraided myself, I still did not have the will to turn around and put the man's needs before my own.

The meeting began with worship, but although the Vineyard songs were truly beautiful and passionate, I could not get the poor homeless man out of my mind and was consumed by the thought that I had completely failed him. When the worship finished, John Wimber stood on the stage and invited us to meet a very special person. To my astonishment, it was the homeless man. One of John Wimber's team was apparently walking behind me on the Thames Embankment. Unlike me, he stopped and spoke to the man. The man shared his story and his plight and allowed himself to be prayed for. He gave a short testimony of response to being rescued. John Wimber made him feel like royalty and the parable of the Good Samaritan came flooding to mind, I felt a complete identification with the priest and the Levite who passed by the man beaten by the robbers without coming to his aid. I made a promise to the Lord that I would never repeat such abject failure again.

One of the most impressive lessons I learnt was the model of prayer ministry that was used. There were none of the excesses I had come to associate with some of the more notable churches in America. There was no shouting in prayer or the choreographed raising of emotions. The personal dignity of those receiving prayer was maintained throughout. The members of the ministry team did not draw attention to themselves and the worship team played gently and with reverence as people were receiving prayer ministry. There was a tangible sense of the presence of God that was awe inspiring and produced a lasting impression on many, including myself.

Whilst driving home after the week's conference, I began to listen to one of the Vineyard worship CDs that I had bought. The music captivated me as I had never heard anything quite like it before. It seemed to open up my soul and as I drove I felt overwhelmed by the love and mercy of a God who was allowing me to experience a truly wonderful level of intimacy with Him. The next motorway service station couldn't come soon enough as I wanted to bathe in this experience without the distraction of having to concentrate on driving. Just as I parked, the next track came on. It was a song composed by Danny Daniels and it contained the words,

> I am a wounded soldier,
>
> But I will not leave the fight
> Because the Great Physician is healing me.
> So I'm standing in the battle in the armour of His light,
> Because His mighty power is real in me.

I certainly felt like a wounded soldier as my personal faults and failures were brought sharply into focus at the Conference. But I also knew I was a work in progress. I had known the healing touch of the Lord and was acutely aware of the need for further encounters of life-changing grace. As the tears flowed yet again, I rededicated my life to Christ; to the spiritual battle in my own personal life, and to the bruises that inevitably come to those Christians who choose to present the Gospel in both Word and deed. Saint Paul beautifully illustrated these truths as he was determined to present the Gospel in Word and deed. In writing to the Church at Corinth, he declared,

> *"My message and my preaching were not with wise and persuasive words, but with a demonstration of the Spirit's power, so that your faith might not rest on men's wisdom, but on God's power."*

1 Corinthians 2:4,5

With regards to the bruises received in Christian ministry, Paul wrote,

> *"I consider that our present sufferings are not worth comparing with the glory that will be revealed to us."*

Romans 8:18

These Scriptures became both a bedrock and an inspiration for my life in Christ.

16

Kingdom Faith Ministries

I had an insatiable appetite to learn more about the ministry of healing and the person and work of the Holy Spirit. My thirst for knowledge and experience was unquenchable and I regularly sought the Lord in days of prayer for insight and direction. Each time I read a book about healing and the work of the Holy Spirit, I would ask the Lord if there was anything in the life and ministries of the authors that He wanted me to pursue further.

In the early 1980s, I read the book by Colin Urquhart entitled *When the Spirit Comes*. The book detailed the wonderful story of what happened when Colin was the vicar of St Hugh's, Lewsey, in Luton. My spirit soared as I read the book. This was closely followed by reading publications written by Charles Sibthorpe and Bob Gordon. All three of these authors had worked together at The Hyde in East Sussex. It was here that Kingdom Faith Ministries flourished. It was such a blessing to read of a church leadership that had also developed a thirst for discovering more about our inheritance in Christ and the resources He had established through the gifts and ministries of the Holy Spirit. Over a period of time we were able to send our leaders to The Hyde for teaching, encouragement and personal ministry. As a consequence of these close links with Kingdom Faith Ministries, we invited them to come to South Wales to lead a mission at Swansea University, the team being led by Charles Sibthorpe. It was an incredible joy and privilege to be a part of this mission in which many Christians were introduced to well balanced teaching and life-changing experiences of the Holy Spirit at work.

During my own visit to The Hyde, I spent some time with Charles Sibthorpe and shared my vision of increasing the leadership team at Christchurch. I had felt in prayer that the new member would probably be English and female and asked Charles if any of the Hyde community were potentially available for moving on. He did not know when he suggested the possibility of a woman called Sandy, that God had already showed her it was time to leave the 'greenhouse' of The Hyde and be 'planted out' in the wider world.

A short while later Sandy and I visited the Bishop's Palace in Llandaff as, in order to offer her a salaried full-time appointment, I needed to gain permission from Bishop Roy, our diocesan Bishop. He was absolutely marvellous as he listened intently to the story of how we came to know Sandy and why we felt this situation was a God-given opportunity for the parish to substantially progress. I am glad he asked why it was that we felt that the appointing of Sandy was right for us and rather than a curate. An outline of her credentials and experience was enough to convince him that a curate would need a number of years to be trained to such a level. Sandy had significant administrative gifts with an overlay of profound spirituality.

Bishop Roy took to Sandy very quickly and was not even deterred when she said that she was Baptist! He refused to accept this as a problem and offered her a private Confirmation service in his small chapel in the Bishop's Palace. We were both completely taken aback by this and even more surprised when he asked about Sandy's accommodation. He wasn't impressed with the arrangements we had proposed and said as far as he was concerned she should be regarded as a curate and as a consequence he was going to ask the 'powers that be' to purchase a house for her. This was completely unprecedented and was one of the factors which led Bishop Roy to say later that women with vocations to serve, such as Sandy, would one day be offered Ordination. It was in fact just eleven years later that the first women were ordained in the Church in Wales in January 1997.

Sandy proved to be an enormous blessing to the parish, but no one was more blessed than I. Here was a Christian whose leadership qualities were quite exceptional. Every time I let her down, she would come to me and we would talk it through and pray together. She was never afraid to share her concerns or questions in private. Her loyalty was exemplary and this provided a much needed safety net for me in which I could offload when under pressure and seek wisdom and perspective for plans and aspirations.

Another lady from The Hyde came to visit Sandy some eighteen months after she had joined us. She was a mature woman of prayer, with a great deal of parish experience through her work as a member of the Church Army. During her visit I had a strong leading of the Spirit to invite her also to come to Merthyr. She agreed and subsequently worked here as well as taking up a position as a District Nurse. Not long after she arrived she began to enjoy sharing her love of walking and enjoying the countryside with Bob. Bob, as I wrote earlier, was the man who had been an atheist and wonderfully converted as a result of the 'onion' prayers of his late wife Joan. They duly fell in love and experienced a marriage that proved to be a source of great blessing to all those privileged to know them and to receive prayer and ministry from them.

The 'Saints Alive' course gave Sandy the ideal context in which she could be a mother hen with her chicks. Members were invited to her home for meals and this started a chain reaction that caught on. It was the use of this course which successfully encouraged a good number of our congregation to experience the Baptism in the Holy Spirit and Spiritual Gifts. The Church became much more 'homely' as many members copied her example. One Sunday, when it had been snowing, an elderly member slipped and injured her back. Sandy prayed for the Lord to heal the lady's back and there was an instant response as the pain left and full mobility was restored. On another occasion, I was called away from taking a Healing Service in church in order to go to a local viaduct where a young man was threatening to commit suicide. Sandy was reluctantly drafted in and although she was nervous, she led the service and a number of those who attended testified to profound blessings being received.

After running the Saints Alive course for a few years, the next stage of the spiritual progression of the church came when we established a link with the parish of Hawkwell, in Essex that was led by Tony and Patricia Higton. By the grace of God, they had transformed the parish to be a centre of renewal. Their experiences resulted in them producing a 12 week discipleship course which was followed by a 12 week commitment course. These courses detailed the component parts for the outworking of the vision and values for a church wanting to work out with a practical dynamic the implications of being a Spirit-filled community of believers. A growing number of parishes were being transformed as a result of their connection to Hawkwell and Tony and Patricia spent a considerable amount of their time visiting and encouraging those churches throughout the country.

It was a particularly challenging and painful time for me personally when Tony came to Christchurch. During his visit, a time was set aside for members of the church to have an appointment with him. Members were told they could ask for personal spiritual direction as well as share their perspective about how the church was being led. The comments concerning the leading of the church were collated and Tony went through them with me, one at a time in the presence of the Parochial Church Council. This was done at my request as I wanted to demonstrate my openness to criticism and accountability to the leadership team. Indeed, this was in response to one of the many teachings that we all signed up to having completed the Commitment Course produced by Tony and Patricia. As Tony went through the criticisms, my heart sank. I knew the perceptions were true. Waves of emotion came over me. I felt sadness, guilt, failure and incompetence. It was as if these feelings had voices and they were all condemning me and urging me to resign there and then. Fortunately, I recognised these 'voices' as temptations that often ride on the back of personal criticisms with the intention of producing a response that would be regretted later. I was so pleased I held my tongue because the leaders could see that I was crestfallen and they spoke words of encouragement and love that made a deep impression on me and ministered to my discouragement.

As I reflected on this experience in the days that followed I sensed the Lord saying to me that He doesn't demand perfection in the lives of those He calls to leadership, but He does demand faith. So I read again the Scriptures concerning the lives of such leaders as Abraham, Moses, and King David. They were all commended for their faith and yet they all exhibited significant failings in their personal lives. The question I needed to ask was, in the light of the meeting with Tony, could my leadership team still work with me. To my great relief and gratitude I found they said they could and they did! In fact, it became clear to them that I was being increasingly called to minister to other churches together with a ministry team.

At meetings of the Parochial Church Council, we had wonderful times of ministering to each other one by one with prayer for healing, a prophetic word or simple encouragement. The presence of the Holy Spirit was occasionally very powerful indeed. At one of the meetings, one of our leaders was unable to be with us as he was having a severe bout of pain as a consequence of a long standing spinal injury. Whilst talking briefly about the situation, we felt led by the Holy Spirit to suspend our meeting and several of our leaders went to Peter's house to pray for him. Those that remained behind entered into a time of prayer for him to be healed. Peter had a wonderful faith and was a veritable sponge whenever he received prayer. He welcomed us with open arms when we told him we had suspended our meeting as we felt led by the Holy Spirit to minister to him. We prayed for Peter and he was gloriously healed and the new strength of his spine proved to be a great and powerful testimony to many people who heard his story. I believe the delivery of the Commitment Course produced at Hawkwell, went a very long way to produce the maturity necessary in our leaders for unity and love to be maintained amongst us and for the Holy Spirit to take us deeper into our inheritance in Christ.

There is no doubting the fact that I often let the discovery of new ideas for ministry and church development supersede my relationships with people. However, I was blessed with quality leaders who supported me and who ably filled several of the gaps I left which would normally be expected of a vicar. I was enormously grateful to them for their maturity in leading house groups and pastoring new converts. They provided much of the spiritual glue that kept us all together and enabled meaningful fellowship to take place. When it came to the 'Passing of the Peace' during the Sunday morning Communion Service, there was so much hugging and blessing taking place it was often difficult to resume the service.

A good number of people gave their lives to Christ at our church services whilst others received calls to vocations. However, our church never grew considerably in numbers and I often felt more like a headmaster of a school. As fast as new people arrived, others were leaving to go elsewhere. I have to admit I often experienced a measure of disappointment and sadness as members of the church left to become ordained or to be a blessing to the Church in other contexts. It wasn't a case of me wanting to have the reputation of leading a large church but rather one of a struggle to realise and accept the Lord was calling us to be a 'sending' church. Robert, Chris, Huw and Ceirion all became priests, whilst others left to join missionary organisations or other churches. My consolation was to be found in the knowledge they were being a source of great blessing wherever they were called to minister.

17

The Season of Pilgrimages

In the 1980s I led several pilgrimages to the Holy Land including one from the parish as well as a Diocesan pilgrimage. The company that I favoured was *Holy Land Christian Travel* as they provided excellent preparation and allowed me to go on a Familiarisation Tour before leading a group of pilgrims myself. Whilst on the Familiarisation Tour, there were three experiences that made a great impression on me.

The first was in Jerusalem. The company commissioned a lecturer to take us on a tour of the city and he explained the architectural significance of the many buildings and artefacts we were shown. The lecturer stood on the steps of the Southern Wall Excavations and read out the speech of Peter recorded in Acts 2:14-41. He prefaced the reading by stating that Jerusalem was the only capital city in the world that was not built alongside a river and for many years so-called biblical scholars had disputed whether the Bible had accurately recorded the event because of this fact. Verse 41 states, *"Those who accepted this message were baptised, and about three thousand were added to their number that day"*. The question that had puzzled scholars for many years was, if there was no river in Jerusalem, then how could the disciples have baptised three thousand converts in a single day. On the face of it it seemed as if it was impossible. However, when the Southern Wall Excavations began in 1967, the archeologists discovered enormous steps that led up to Temple Mount stretching 922 feet in length. At the base of the steps were dozens of ritual baths called *mikvah*. Their purpose was to purify those who wanted to enter the Temple Mount. The *mikvah* were constructed as two sets of separated stairs; the stairs going down were for those seeking ritual purification by immersion in the water and the stairs going up led the purified to the steps leading to Temple Mount. Thousands of worshippers and pilgrims would have been able to be purified in this way in a single day. Jesus Himself would have used a *mikvah* before entering Temple Mount and the disciples would have been able to use these *mikvah* to baptise the three thousand people who heard the speech of Peter and wanted to be baptised there and then.

The lesson that I learnt from this explanation of how the three thousand converts were baptised in a day was a salutary one. The healthy way of dealing with a biblical text that seems to defy explanation is to say just that – it defies a contemporary explanation. Many biblical scholars have fallen foul of the temptation to force a conclusion by stating that the bible contains inaccuracies and contradictions. In such circumstances some scholars elevate their own fallible understanding above the infallible Word of God which does indeed contain a number of puzzling texts.

The second experience of great significance that I had was when I visited the Dead Sea. On the way there, the guide reached into his bag and took out what he said was 'manna' – the food that was provided by God to sustain the Israelites during their forty years in the wilderness of Sinai. The guide went on to explain that the manna that he was holding was the result of a secretion from the Tamarisk tree that is commonly found in the Sinai desert. He said that desert beetles insert their proboscises into the stem of the Tamarisk trees so as to feed at night time. This sets up a capillary action and the stem oozes manna. The manna then drops off the stem and that is what the Israelites found when they woke up in the morning.

This all seemed very plausible to me at the time and I took it at face value to be the truth. I even told my congregation back home that this was the explanation. How wrong I was! On a subsequent visit to Israel a Jewish guide informed me that such explanations of manna appearing in the wilderness fly in the face of the facts. He said that the so-called 'manna' does indeed come from secretions from the Tamarisk tree, but is only produced from mid-May to the end of July, and hence does not appear all year long as described in Exodus 16. He also said that if you add up the number of Israelites that entered the Sinai desert as described by the census recorded in Numbers 1, then there would have been, as a conservative estimate, about two million people. The total output of Tamarisk 'manna' for an entire season of secretions would not have fed the Israelites for a single day. Finally, he asked me to read Exodus 16:31 and Numbers 11:7-8. These verses state, *"The people of Israel called the bread manna. It was like coriander seed and tasted like wafers made with honey,"* and *"The manna was like coriander seed and looked like resin. The people went round gathering it, and then ground it in a handmill or crushed it in a mortar. They cooked it in a pot or made it into cakes. And it tasted like something made with olive oil"*. The Tamarisk 'manna' is not grainy and is unable to be crushed or to be used to make bread.

Again, this was a good lesson to learn. I have no problem at all in believing in the miraculous but I had accepted an explanation from the school of Biblical Rationalism that seeks to provide natural explanations for all miraculous events. If I had done further research I would have discovered the truth that the manna that God provided for the Israelites was a unique and miraculous provision.

The third experience I had on the Familiarisation Tour was truly remarkable. We were visiting the Church of the Beatitudes near the shore of Lake Galilee when I saw two people fall over. They were about two hundred yards from the church and had gone down to have a closer look at the lake. I went to find out what had happened and to help them as they seemed to be in quite some distress. Another couple, who were closer than I, also saw them and rushed to their aid. When they got to them, they too fell down. When I got there, I fell down. The sense of the presence of Jesus and His utter holiness was completely overwhelming and the five of us were just lying there in awe and tearfulness. It was an experience I will never forget. Time seemed to stand still. It was as if we had entered into a portal from heaven. Eventually, we crawled away from the spot on our hands and knees. Within a few yards we were back in the natural realm of things. Stunned and hardly able to speak, we went our separate ways.

The next time I visited the Church of the Beatitudes, I was the leader of the party. One of our group was a committed atheist and the only reason he had come on the pilgrimage was because he wanted to go on the boat ride across Galilee. As we were setting up for a short service outside, I recalled what had happened to me the last time I was there. I wondered if it was just a one off experience or could it be that, whatever it was, was still there? Nothing ventured nothing gained, so I asked him to go to the spot, explaining it was a good place from which to take a lovely photograph of Lake Galilee. The rest of the group were singing a hymn when I noticed that he had fallen down with his head cupped in his hands. I couldn't wait for the service to end. When we finished, I asked his wife to follow me and we went towards her husband. By this time he was coming to meet us. He looked ashen. His wife asked him what had happened. He told her he had met Jesus and that He was real after all. They held each other in their arms and sobbed. Later, at the hotel, I asked him if he could tell me what he had experienced. He said he did not have words to adequately describe what happened. It was as if he had taken a step out of this world and into another. He didn't see Jesus but sensed that He was all around him, enveloping him in both love and acceptance. No words were exchanged in the encounter, but disbelief was exchanged for faith, and he subsequently became a Christian.

A similar experience happened a couple of years later. On this occasion, one of the party, who was not a Christian, became ill on the eve of the day we were due to go to the Church of the Beatitudes followed by the boat ride across Lake Galilee. He insisted that he would not be left behind in the hotel as this day in the itinerary was to be the highlight of the tour as far as he was concerned. Once again, when we arrived at the Church of the Beatitudes, I directed him to the area where the encounters had taken place. He didn't want to go too far from the group and so he stood about fifty yards away. We were part of the way through our open air service when he suddenly froze and then lifted his arms in the air for several seconds before lowering them and standing motionless. After the service, his wife went up to him and asked how he was feeling. He told her that he had been healed. He said that it was as if time slackened pace to slow motion and he felt something gradually pass him from right to left. Firstly, his right ear became unblocked; then his right eye; then the puffiness in the gland in the right of his neck subsided, then his nose became unblocked, and so the experience continued until all the pain and swellings had gone. He said he felt a slight movement of air that was disturbed as Jesus walked by. He was convinced that it was Jesus who had healed him and no one tried to disenfranchise him from his view. When he got back home, he was baptised in the Chapel that his wife was attending in Penarth and they continued to worship together.

In 1989, I led a combined Pilgrimage for members of Cyfarthfa Church and the parish of Dowlais. There is no doubt that the experience of a Pilgrimage to the Holy Land can be quite intense. With each visit to a Holy Site, the Bible comes alive in a vibrant way and there are many deeply moving moments. Nevertheless, in between these spiritual impacting experiences, there are also moments of great mirth.

On one day in Jerusalem, our group met up with a wonderful black Pentecostal Bishop from London and members of his church. Most of them dwarfed our party. When it came to the crossing of the main road outside the Damascus Gate members of his Church just walked into the road and put up their hands for the traffic to stop. Startled motorists initially sounded their horns. Then there was silence as they gazed at the sight of the huge imposing characters that had stopped all the traffic. We all trooped across the road like little school children obeying several giant lollipop men at a school crossing.

If that wasn't embarrassing enough, far worse was to follow when we got to the hotel. The Bishop and his entourage decided to have an impromptu service with us. Before the service began, the Bishop said to the tiny Muslim bartender that the bar was now closed. Not realising who he was dealing with, he replied that the bar was in fact open. The Bishop then signalled to one of his members by the name of Jake to close the bar. Jake walked into the bar and standing alongside the bartender, with his arm around him, he asked him if the bar was still open. This time the bartender gave the right answer and said that the bar was closed. Then the Bishop started the service. I have to say that it was nothing like any of us had ever experienced before. There were loud prayers and incantations, singing in tongues, prophecies, and extemporised songs that were made up from their experiences that day. Then the Bishop told our party to form a circle and they would form a circle facing us. They were going to Pass the Peace with us – but not like any Passing of the Peace that we had known. We were to stay still and their circle would move in a clockwise direction so that each one of them would Pass the Peace with each one of us. Many of the Bishop's group were over six feet tall and double our average weight. Standing in front of me was a large lady whose breasts were at the same height as my head. She clasped me with her arms and suddenly, not only could I not see or hear anything but I couldn't breathe, such was the passion she so lovingly showed me. By the time they had finished Passing the Peace, most of us needed resuscitation. We laughed about it later, but at the time some of us felt as if we were fighting for our lives!

The hotel we were staying in was not the best to say the least. Basil Fawlty's hotel was like the Hilton in comparison. The food was traditional food for Israel and bore little resemblance to what we were used to back home. Poor Bryn, he really struggled. There was no way that he could eat the food and he would say at every mealtime that he was looking forward to the Red Cross food parcels arriving.

One evening, whilst we were in the dining room, the lights went out. It was only when the candles came out that we noticed there were up to ten plugs in a single socket. We were invited to remain seated whilst the chef prepared cold courses for the meal.

In the gloom, the person sitting next to Bryn asked him why he wasn't eating. Bryn said that as he looked at his plate there was something looking back at him and there was no way that he was going to eat a single thing. When the courses of cold food stopped arriving, the chef presented himself in the dining room and said that he hoped we had enjoyed the meal in the circumstances. A ripple of applause began and Bryn whispered loudly, "For Pete's sake don't clap him or he'll bring us some more."

On leaving the hotel that night, some of us went to a local coffee shop. We were looking for some food for Bryn, but there was none in the shop. Bryn's grandson, Darren, said that it was not safe for Bryn to go wandering late at night in search of food so he would go for him. He left the cafe and turned right. We were all getting anxious as Darren took ages to return. When he got back he was carrying a large bar of Cadbury's chocolate with nuts. Bryn asked Darren how it took him so long and where did he eventually find the chocolate. Darren said that he walked all around the walls of Jerusalem and found the chocolate in the shop next to the coffee shop – on the left.

The following day we travelled into the Judaean desert to visit the Dead Sea and the Herodian palace-fortress at Masada. I was at the front of the bus with the guide, when the driver radioed the bus company to say that there was something wrong with the engine of the bus and they might have to send a replacement.

I could hear the driver being asked what was wrong with the bus. The driver explained that every time it went round a bend there was a strange noise coming from the engine. Everybody on the bus was then told there was a problem with the bus when we went round bends. Gasps and laughter came from the back of the bus. Bryn did not have his false teeth in, and he had sucked the chocolate from the remains of his Cadbury's Chocolate Nut bar and surreptitiously put the nuts on the floor of the bus. We all had a game of 'hunt the nuts' until we had rounded up all the culprits.

The driver was not best pleased as was evidenced by his verbal report to the bus company that the problem was resolved.

After visiting Masada we went to the Dead Sea for a swim. Swimming is a misnomer when it comes to the Dead Sea. The water is so impregnated with salt that it is too dangerous to even attempt to swim properly. As you walk into the sea there is the strangest sensation of the water pushing you upwards and before you get to chest height the water has taken over and it is impossible to stand. We had been warned that it was very important to make use of the outside shower afterwards so as to get all the salt off the nether regions in particular. An orderly queue was formed and it was Peter's turn next to shower. Suddenly, Haydn pulled open the back of Peter's trunks and told him to get some water down there. In a flash the onlookers were treated to what seemed like an excerpt from a Tom and Jerry cartoon. Peter took off like a shot, with Haydn holding tightly onto the back of Peter's trunks. When Haydn finally let go of the trunks, Peter seemed jet propelled as he hurtled towards the bus. When we arrived back at the hotel, you could tell that Peter had not completed his shower by the way he walked with ramrod stiff legs, much to the amusement of all of us.

Prior to this Pilgrimage, Sandy had started dating John. He and I were sharing a room and we spoke at length about his relationship with Sandy and whether they should get married. We decided to prayerfully ask the Lord to give a clear confirmation if it was His will or not. The following Sunday morning John subsequently prayed privately that if one of the hymns was *How Great Thou Art* then he would ask Sandy to marry him. For some reason, they did not sit with the main pilgrimage group but in a small section of seating a short distance away from the tomb where the service was taking place at the Garden Tomb. After the initial announcements, the leader of the service then announced that the first hymn was *How Great Thou Art*. Truly amazing! After the service, John and Sandy stood and looked over the entrance of the tomb and he proposed to her. She said 'yes' and they were soon married. They have two very gifted children and continue to be a source of great blessing to all those who seek their ministry, prayer and support.

There is no doubt that going on a Pilgrimage together as a Church can create deep and lasting friendships, and be a great blessing to the spiritual growth of both individuals and the Church as a family of believers.

Healing, Heartache and Humour

18

Choral and Wedding Bloopers

Jim and his wife Margaret were also members of the church choir and at Christmastide the choir, augmented by other members of the church, would sing carols in the streets and visit the nursing homes in the area.

On one occasion, we were invited to sing carols and conduct a short service at a nearby nursing home. The residents were all sat at large round tables with a glass of orange juice each. All was going well when one of the residents, without looking, went to take hold of her orange juice. She knocked the glass over and let out a gasp. Alas, she let out more than a gasp. She let out her false teeth as well. They began to disappear to the other side of the table riding on the wave of orange juice. Before the teeth fell on the floor and bit the dust, Margaret, seeing this unholy sight, immediately leapt to the rescue. She grabbed the dentures and quickly returned them – to the wrong resident, who promptly put them in her own mouth. The lady whose teeth disappeared into the wrong mouth then clambered onto the table and tried to force open the jaws of the alien host. It was all over in a flash and Margaret retrieved the dentures and returned them to the rightful owner – who promptly put them back into her mouth. Now it is at times like this that a wave of ridiculous and inappropriate humour often sweeps over me. On this occasion I asked if we could change the next hymn to *"Oh 'Gum' All Ye Faithful"*! I was appropriately reprimanded for having such bad taste.

It never ceased to amaze me that no matter how much time was spent with couples and their families on wedding preparations and rehearsals, there was nevertheless such a rich variety of hilarious mishaps that would have provided the writers of *The Vicar of Dibley* with great material.

The bride arrived in church to a trumpet fanfare. As she walked down the aisle escorted by her proud father, the male guests' heads turned at the sight of the immaculate bride. Several of their partners gently reminded their men with a sharp elbow into the ribcage to close their mouths at this jaw dropping sight. Her bridal veil and tiara decorated her long, golden ringlets. Her dress had a bridal train and long flowing sleeves.

The service went smoothly until we came to the part where the bride's father gives the bride away. In the rehearsal, the father had been shown how to take the bride's left hand by simply reaching across the front of the bride. Her poor Dad was already showing signs of nerves when he decided to step between the bride and groom in the vain attempt to take her hand. With his left foot, he trod on the bridal veil and this had the disastrous effect of yanking her golden ringlet hairpiece totally off her head. There were gasps of horror from the congregation. Dad, now gripped by panic, then swung across his right foot and trod on the long flowing sleeve of her dress. This had the effect of propelling her right arm down and backwards. Her elbow landed safely in the stomach of her father. He was so winded that he ended up on the floor holding her stomach. The bride's mother, full of compassionate understanding for her husband was heard to shout, "I am going to kill him". Just in case he had not heard it the first time, she kindly repeated herself. The poor bride now looked more like the bride of Frankenstein with normal hair now revealing all manner of curlers and clips giving a dishevelled look to a face that had tear filled mascara running down it. Many of the ladies in the congregation held their heads and gasped in horror, but just as many of the men held their hands to their mouths in a desperate attempt to muffle their raucous laughter. The scene was one of utter chaos from which there was no dignified redemption.

It was certainly not one of my finest moments as ridiculous humorous thoughts kept invading my mind. At the end of the service I always invite the husband to kiss his bride. The thought came to me, "David, you may kiss the bride (or would you prefer to have her cleaned up first!)"

On another occasion, the bride was extremely large to say the least. The athlete, Colin Jackson, had been to a wedding in our church a few months before, and I should have asked for his contact details. He would have come in very handy at the wedding rehearsal as he could have given the bride's father pew hurdling lessons because the aisle could only just accommodate the bride who had a lovely personality and was a really bubbly person.

During the preparations, she told me that she hoped nothing would go wrong in the service as she had a weird sense of humour and that she could burst out in laughter at the drop of a hat. I shrugged this off at the time and assured her that I would be speaking softly to the couple throughout the service so that they would not be left to remember anything that was to happen in the rehearsal. All went well until we got to the announcement of the final hymn. The couple at that time were kneeling at the altar rail. The intercessions had been completed and the organist pressed the button for the organ to start. The organ made an horrendous sound as the plunger was sucked back into the organ. The bride did an impression of Ted Heath as her shoulders started to rhythmically move up and down. Thankfully, she managed to control herself. I explained to the congregation that we had a slight technical hitch with the organ, but that the last hymn was very well known and we would sing it unaccompanied. At that moment, the organ came back to life and the plunger came down, making a dreadful sound. The bride's shoulders started to shake again. However, on this occasion, there was no going back. With a belly laugh that could be heard miles away, she keeled over and was spread-eagled on her back. I thought the choir stalls were in danger as she thrashed about from right to left whilst holding her stomach and laughing uncontrollably. It was the sort of belly laugh that was absolutely infectious and we all joined in, myself included.

After about a minute, I composed myself and asked the bridegroom how long his new bride would be in this state. He calmly looked at his watch and said very slowly, "Well…about ten to fifteen minutes." Horrified by this, I then stupidly said to the bridegroom, "Can you pick her up?" to which he replied, "Not b….. likely! I'm not going to get a hernia on my wedding day." At that, I burst out in laughter once again. After regaining a modicum of control, I asked if he could gather a few of his friends to carry her out to the vestry. The friends he identified nervously accepted the invitation to come to his aid. Whilst she was in the vestry for what seemed like an age, one could hear sudden bursts of laughter interspersed between coughing, chuckling and throat clearing. Eventually, she emerged, but attempts to remove the mascara stains on her face left her looking like a koala bear. Fortunately she took it all in her stride, but I did wonder if she would have another attack during the reception.

Most wedding couples have never had the experience of being the centre of attention and having to speak publicly, so it is not surprising that they are usually quite nervous. However, one couple was particularly nervous and totally flustered even at the rehearsal.

I reassured them, as I did with all wedding couples that I would be speaking to them throughout the service and they would not have to remember a single thing from the rehearsal. During the service, I took great pains to explain everything to them at every stage. After the exchanging of vows at the chancel step, I asked them to kneel for the blessing of their marriage prayers. I then asked them to follow me to the altar rail for the intercessions. I turned and walked slowly towards the altar, and as I did, members of the choir were bowing their heads and covering their mouths trying unsuccessfully not to giggle. I could hear a strange noise from behind me. It was the sound of the tearing of material. When I reached the altar, I turned around and was horrified to see the couple crawling on their hands and knees because I had not told them to stand. As the bride struggled to crawl, her stiletto heels were tearing her petticoats to shreds. I had to cover my face with the service leaflet as I could not keep a straight face. When they finally presented themselves to the altar rail for the intercessions they told me that they only realised their mistake when they looked at the faces of the choir. Then the bridegroom said that rather than look silly they decided to complete the crawl in the hope that the congregation would think it was part of the service. At the end of the service I told the congregation that I hoped they would enjoy the reception but equally hoped that it would prove to be as rip roaring a time as it had been in church!

When I think of some of the things that went wrong at weddings, I am sure there would have been a considerable sum of money to be made by the church if the videos had been sent to such television programmes as *It'll Be Alright On The Night.* In one wedding, all the guests started to laugh when the bridegroom knelt down. On the soles of his shoes someone had written 'TOO LATE', whilst at another wedding the bride's garter fell down her leg. Instead of stepping out of it she walked as if she had a wooden leg whilst dragging her heel on the floor. It was reminiscent of the John Cleese sketch of the *Ministry of Funny Walks.* At another wedding, the bridegroom and best man hired a tandem bicycle to ride to the church. They had not got very far when the bicycle developed a flat tyre. By the time they arrived at the church they were exhausted and in great need of a strong deodorant.

Then there was the wedding when the bride arrived at church without her flowers. They had been left at her parents' house. The best man and a friend sped off in a car to get the flowers as it was only a couple of miles away. When they got there, the house was of course locked and in the panic they had not brought the house key. Undaunted, the friend broke a window and the best man went in to get the flowers. In the meantime a neighbour saw what was happening and called the police. The police arrived and promptly arrested both of the men. They pleaded with the police to take them to the church so that the bride's father could verify their story. They were either the best dressed burglars the police had ever seen or they were genuine in their story. Thankfully, the police took them to the church and the bride's father initially said that he had never seen them before in his life before pausing and confirming their story.

Now and again I came across the archetypal best man who does not need telling what to do because he has done it all before. They set off alarm bells in me and I always know that there is going to be a gaffe coming up. At one wedding, when it came to the signing of the registers in the vestry, I had asked the best man to ensure that the witnesses were brought into the vestry following the bridal party. As the bride took her seat to sign the registers, the parents of both parties arrived, then the bridesmaids and page boys, then followed uncles and aunties and guests. We were so crammed in the vestry that the bride was so hunched over the registers that it was impossible for her to write. I appealed to people to stop trying to cram into the vestry. In the end the verger opened the external vestry door from the outside to let me out together with many of the oxygen starved family and friends. I rushed around to the front door of the church and all I could hear was the know-it-all best man still ushering the congregation through the vestry door with the encouraging words, "Anyone else wanting to witness the signing of the registers just join the queue to the vestry". Hurrying to where the best man had stationed himself, I asked him if he was a fan of the *Dr Who* programmes. When he asked what I meant by this, I said that the vestry was not a Tardis and that it was proving difficult to fit over a hundred people in a space where ten people would be a congested crowd. I decided to resort to humour but it was not at all what I felt like saying to him.

Lastly, there was a wedding that was ruined by a horse. The bride had hired a horse and carriage to transport her and her father to the church. All was going well and she set off in plenty of time before the wedding. Sadly, the horse lost a shoe as it descended a long hill. The horse limped at a snail's pace and they were never going to make it in time. When they were a quarter of an hour late a search party was sent out to find them. They came back to the church with the news that they were on their way but the horse was struggling as it had lost a shoe. The bride refused the offer of a lift in the car that was sent to find her. Three quarters of an hour late, the bride and her father finally arrived. However, she insisted on having her photograph taken in front of the horse and carriage together with her father and bridesmaids. Equine revenge then reared its ugly head. As the photograph was being taken the horse brayed and sprayed all those assembled with saliva. I was standing at the door of the church when I heard the screams and cries as they all rushed away from the horse and came running towards me. The bride's mother decided to take a collection – of all the tissues that the congregation was able muster so as to clean up the mess as best they could. The service eventually started an hour late, but I was contented that the horse had had the last laugh. If the horse was trying to make her look very 'foalish' it certainly succeeded.

19

Bishop Chiu Ban It takes our Healing Experience to Another Level

Bishop Chiu Ban It of Singapore came to visit us at Christchurch for a long weekend. He told us that even after he had become a Christian, he still felt that there was something very important that was lacking in his life and he would never experience true fulfilment without this missing link. He struggled with depression and self-deprecation and was molested with thoughts of suicide during his desperate search for what he was missing. As he shared his testimony with us he told us that on one occasion he walked onto the Clifton Suspension Bridge at Bristol with the intention of jumping off. What made it all the more distressing was he did not know what it was that he was searching for. All he knew was that he craved for whatever it was and he prayed in desperation for God to give him a revelation, an insight, anything so that he could receive what his spirit was pining for.

Then, in December 1972, whilst attending a World Council of Churches meeting in Bangkok his spiritual quest was realised. He was taking a shower in his hotel room when all of a sudden he began singing in tongues as he felt an inrush of the presence of God in his body. From that moment on, he was a changed man. He began to hold healing services in his cathedral in Singapore and many people were being healed. Shortly afterwards, he partnered with Canon James Wong and between them they saw a great outpouring of grace as Charismatic Renewal spread throughout Singapore and South East Asia. He then felt led by

God to visit all the areas of his diocese. Going from place to place he preached the Gospel and healed the sick. So many people were being healed and becoming Christians that he had to appoint a priest to organise a ministry team that went to all the places where Bishop Chiu Ban It had been so as to prepare the converts for Baptism and Confirmation. He told us story after story of what God was doing in his Diocese and understood that what he had been missing in his life was the experience of the Baptism in the Holy Spirit. He now felt anointed by God to preach *and* heal.

By the time it came to the Sunday evening service there was a great sense of expectancy in the church. The time of worship was wonderful and you just knew that the Lord was with us in a very special way. Then came the time to invite people to come forward for prayer. Picture the scene if you will. The Bishop was sat in the Bishop's chair between the choir stalls. He was dressed in his robes and at his side was a church member acting as his chaplain and carrying his crook and mitre. A man came forward with a built up shoe. The Bishop asked him what he should pray for. The man said he had contracted polio as a child and his one leg was several inches shorter than the other. The Bishop then called for a chair so that the man could sit facing him. He asked the man to take off his built up shoe and place his feet on the Bishop's lap. He did that and it was plain to see how short one of his legs was. The Bishop's chaplain, who was our principal organist at the time, had the best view of all, and was himself a sight to behold.

As the Bishop prayed for the man's leg to grow, the face of the Bishop's chaplain was a picture. His eyes became bulbous and his mouth opened wider and wider whilst taking a larger stance in order to support himself. The leg was growing. The Bishop directed us to continue to worship in song whilst the leg was growing. It seemed an age, but in about ten minutes the withered leg was now the same length as the other leg. We were astounded and in a sense of awe until the man was then asked to return to his seat. He walked as if he was drunk as he struggled to walk properly back to his seat because his legs were now the same length. There were so many lovely things that happened that night I forgot to find out if the man had a lift home. He certainly could not walk in a straight line if he had attempted to put his old built up shoe on again.

Robert, the Bishop's chaplain that night, offered himself for Ordination not long afterwards. He gave up his profession as a history teacher and after being accepted for Ordination found himself in the same college in Llandaff I had attended years earlier. However, he told me when he was asked to give an account of his faith journey, nobody would believe him when he told the story of the visit of Bishop Chiu Ban It to Christchurch, including the healing of the man who had had polio as a child, and experienced his withered leg grow to the same length as his other leg.

Maxine had recently come to faith but had struggled with attendance at church because her husband, Ian, was not a Christian and often wanted to do other things with his family on a Sunday. I had encouraged her not to fret about this and to pray in faith that Ian would eventually also come to faith. He had always said if he ever came to faith then he would have to have a personal experience that would convince him. In the meantime, I suggested that when Ian wanted to do other things on a Sunday, then she should go along with his wishes so as not to drive a wedge between them.

Ian and his son arrived late at a church barbecue we were having in Cyfarthfa Park and I noticed Ian was limping. I felt a quickening in my spirit and sensed this was a great opportunity. I had a kind of flashback of the man whose leg was lengthened and a surge of faith for Ian's healing. When I asked him what was wrong with his leg, he told me he had torn a ligament and was unable to work. I reminded him of his challenge that he could not believe unless he had an experience of God and asked him if I could pray for his leg. He agreed, and I asked Paul, a leader in our Church plant, to come and pray with me. We both knelt on the grass and placed our hands on Ian's leg. In my mind's eye I envisioned the scene of Bishop Chiu Ban It holding the withered leg of the man who had contracted polio as a child. I thought Paul and I were praying for something far less miraculous. Surely we were praying for the healing of a ligament but in comparison to the lengthening of a leg we were believing for something far less. As we began praying, I became aware how odd this situation must have looked to those standing near us. Then Ian's son said to his dad, "Dad, get them off!" A wave of embarrassment came over me and I quickly finished praying. I then asked Ian if he would test the leg out and let us know how it felt. He flexed his leg gingerly and said he had no pain. He then walked away slowly and that was the last that I saw of him that day.

One of our church members saw Ian coming out of Tesco's the following Monday. He could hardly put one foot in front of the other as he shuffled along. He was asked what was the matter and said he had prayer for his leg the previous Saturday at the church barbecue and there was no pain in his leg afterwards. He couldn't believe he had been healed and so he had spent Sunday in the gym trying to get the pain back. When he woke up on the Monday morning he said he had pain in every part of his body except the leg that had received prayer. This was the experience he had said that he needed and, true to his word, he became a Christian and a member of Christchurch. Ian was a postman and had always had an ambition to become a policeman. Unfortunately, when he applied to the Police Force, he failed the medical examination because of deafness. After receiving prayer ministry, he was healed of the deafness and subsequently passed the medical examination and became a Police Officer.

Another person who insisted he could never become a Christian unless he had an experience was a man who came to the vicarage for marriage preparation. He was a miner who enjoyed bodybuilding as a hobby. Again, I sensed in my spirit this was a great opportunity and so I challenged him to ask the Lord for whatever experience it would take for him to become a Christian. He declined. Undaunted, I told him it was because he was scared. If it wasn't for the fact that I was now feeling full of faith for him, I wouldn't have dared to have been so bold. He insisted he wasn't scared of anyone or anything. I could quite believe it as he had muscles in places most people don't even have places. At this time, he started to puff up his chest, so I asked him to prove to me that he wasn't scared by inviting him to pray a prayer, after me, for a conversion experience. He agreed and prayed with a real sense of challenge to the Lord in his voice. He had followed me in a prayer that challenged the Lord to do whatever it would take to bring this man to faith in Him.

When the couple came back the following week for their next wedding preparation interview, his fiancée nudged him in the ribs and told him to tell me what had happened. His story was literally breathtaking. He was leading his fellow miners towards the coal face when all of a sudden he felt the imprint of a hand on his chest that propelled him backwards, lifting him off his feet and causing several of his friends to lose their balance as he fell into them. Then, all of a sudden, the roof of the mine caved in. When they got to their feet, his friends asked him what caused him to fall back as he did. Without a moment's hesitation, he said he believed it was the hand of the Lord that pushed him in the chest and took him off his feet. He then went on to say that it was the Lord who had saved their lives. He became a changed man after that. If any miners dared to swear or blaspheme when they were on his shift, they would be met with a severe reprimand. I would love to be able to say that after such a dramatic experience he became a Christian, but I cannot. He said that although he was a true believer, he did not want to go any further at that time. I have to admit that my heart sank at his reply. All I could do was to offer him my time in the future if he ever wanted to learn more about what it takes to become a Christian.

The experience of feeling as bold as I did was not my normal persona at all, so when it happens, I am well aware that I am receiving the gift of faith for a particular situation. It is a very rare occurrence for me to receive the gift of faith when I pray for it. It seems to me that it is largely the initiative of the Holy Spirit and I have found that when I receive the gift of faith the prayers I pray in a given situation go up another level – from praying with faith, to praying with a certainty that the Lord is powerfully at work.

One evening, whilst preparing a sermon in my study at the vicarage, the doorbell rang. On opening the door, the well-dressed stranger asked if I could give him advice as he was in a crisis. I invited him in and as soon as he sat down in the study he pulled a gun out of his pocket and told me he wanted all the cash and small valuables that I had in the house. My wife and children were in the lounge next to the study and were oblivious as to what was happening. My heart was in my mouth as I shot up an arrow prayer to the Lord asking for help and mercy. Pointing the gun at me, he said he had fallen on hard times and was desperate. I felt I had to stall for time as I didn't know what to do, so I asked him what had happened to him to resort to such desperate measures as robbing a vicar. As he began to pour out his story, my panic seemed to subside and I was filled with a deep sense of compassion. This puzzled me to begin with, until I realised that the Lord was answering my prayer, so I prayed for the gift of faith for the salvation of the poor man. Suddenly, I was filled with the assurance this was indeed what the Lord wanted and this was his appointed time to be presented with the Gospel. Taking my bible in both hands, I leant towards him and said that what I was holding was far more powerful than his gun, and if he would allow me to explain the bible to him in just five minutes, he could receive enough power to change his life forever. He agreed, and after my five minutes were up, he asked what he would have to do to get the power I was talking about and a new life. I explained that the gun he was pointing at me represented all the bad stuff in his life and the bible I was carrying contained all the promises of the good stuff God wanted him to have. I asked him if he wanted to do an exchange and begin a new life. I offered him my bible and asked him if he was prepared to give up his gun. He paused for several seconds as he considered my offer and then offered me the gun and took my bible.

Almost an hour had passed and I noticed his demeanour had slowly began to change and he began to look quite menacing. I asked him if he had anywhere to stay that night and he told me he didn't as he wasn't from this area. I said if he would allow me to make a telephone call, I could arrange for him to have somewhere to stay that night without having to pay. Breathing a sigh of relief when he agreed, I promptly rang the local police station. I told the Duty Officer who I was and explained I had someone with me who really needed overnight accommodation. The bemused officer asked me if I had the right number. I said I was quite sure I had the correct number and could he ask the manager of the establishment that I needed free overnight accommodation and a good breakfast for someone. I went on to explain that the manager had assured me he also had a car available to take individuals to the accommodation. At last, the penny dropped and the officer asked if I was in trouble. I said thank you very much and asked if a car was available to take the man straight away. Fortunately, the man did not gather from my conversation I had telephoned the police station.

Within minutes, there was a knock at the door and two police officers had arrived. I put my finger to my mouth so that they would not startle the man as the gun was still in the study. I thanked them out loud for being so prompt in sending a car, and whispered into the ear of one of the officers there was a gun on my study desk. They went into the study and one of the officers took the gun whilst the other officer invited the man to come with him. Still holding my bible, the man said that I had tricked him. I told him all I had said to him was true, and if he took the bible with him, he would be able to start his new life in the morning. He protested that he did not understand, and so I reassured him although he did not understand now, in the morning he would.

When they had all left, I went into the lounge and sat down exhausted. Later, I told Marilyn what had happened, and she was horrified that all this had taken place when she and the children were in the room next door. The following morning, I contacted the police and told them that I would not be making any charges against the man. It gave me the opportunity of relating to an officer a full account of what had happened the night before. He seemed very understanding. The man was released from custody that day, still holding my bible. I did want to speak to him, but he left before I got there. I prayed he would make the connection of no charges being brought against him with being forgiven, and also that he would remember our conversation and the prayers we prayed for the beginning of a new life in Christ.

BBC Wales got to hear of what had happened, and one of their reporters, Nicola Smith, came to the house with a film crew to cover the story. This served to give an additional alert to the Church in Wales as to the vulnerability of Vicars and their families as measures were already being taken to increase their security as a result of such dangers.

20

Marilyn's Fight with Illness

In 1980, when Marilyn was thirty nine years old, she was diagnosed with breast cancer. The results of her biopsy were given to us at Velindre Hospital in Cardiff. The staff were amazing. They were well trained to deal with the trauma of such a diagnosis and Dr Webster was so caring and softly spoken as he gave us the news.

We were like rabbits caught in the headlights of a car. It was as if life stood still and remained on pause for several minutes as he explained the treatment regime to us. It didn't sink in as we were so stunned. He recognised this and said that he would explain it all again later. As we travelled home in the car we were still in a state of shock. Marilyn said we must put on a brave face for the sake of the children and let it all sink in before we told them. That night we prayed together and committed ourselves to the love and care of the Lord. I prayed for her healing with great fervour and at length. When I had finished, I was expecting Marilyn to add her prayers for healing but she didn't. Instead she prayed that the Lord would give her enough time to see her children become grown up. I was stunned and became tearful. As we held each other, I asked for her permission to continue praying for her healing every day whilst respecting the fact that her prayers would be quite different. She told me when she prayed for an extension to her life so she could see her children grown up, she felt a great sense of peace that the Lord had answered her prayer and her heart's desire would be granted. I really struggled with this and remember praying and wrestling with the mystery of the grace of God. God's grace is unmerited blessing. It is blessing from God which is more than we desire or deserve. And so I pleaded with God that Marilyn would receive more than she had desired and be completely healed.

Two and a half years later Marilyn discovered a lump in her other breast and she had to have a second mastectomy. The operation went according to plan but there were complications with skin grafts and revisionary surgery leaving her with bouts of severe pain that she hid from those around her. She never questioned her faith and remained convinced of the Lord's promise that she would see her children grown up. Indeed, if anything, her faith grew in spite of her physical condition. She relished opportunities to minister with me and pray for healing. She had a lovely gentle spirit and would often receive Words of Knowledge and encouraging insight and wisdom for those in need.

A further two and a half years later, Marilyn was diagnosed with ovarian cancer. Her condition continued to deteriorate and the time came when she could not take any solid or liquidised foods. She was just able to take sips of water from a spoon. The cancer had spread considerably and it did not seem as if she would see her children grown up after all. Then something truly wonderful happened. During the Sunday evening service we had a time of intercession. Hetty, one of our elderly members said, "I have heard your prayers for Marilyn and I am going to heal her". Then she turned to her friend Peggy and asked her what had just happened. Peggy told her what she had just said. She was astonished, as was the congregation. Hetty was a devout and traditional Anglican who kept her distance from all things charismatic. But the author of all things charismatic was not going to keep His distance from her. His love for her and validation of her faith resulted in the Lord blessing Hetty to say those few words. I remember looking at my watch at the time and wanting the service to be over. I couldn't wait for it to end so I could get back to the vicarage and tell Marilyn what had happened.

When I got home, I rushed up the stairs and sat at Marilyn's bedside and told her what Hetty had said. She then took my hand and asked me at what time did Hetty say those words. I told her and she said at that time she suddenly felt hunger pains and wanted me to come home so she could tell me. I liquidised some food for her and she was able to take it. She gradually regained strength and a year to that day we were given the news at Velindre Hospital that all the cancer had gone. There was great rejoicing amongst family and friends as the good news quickly spread around the country. But Marilyn took me aside and in her softly spoken voice calmly told me that her healing was so her initial prayer could be answered. I protested that surely this was the end of her fight with cancer and that we, as a family, could now look towards the future with a great sense of joy and expectation. She tightened her grip of my hand and looking into my eyes she said, "Steve, it's alright." I knew what she meant and I sensed in my spirit for the first time that she would only live until the Lord had decided that the children had grown up.

Four years later, in 1989, Marilyn became ill again and was diagnosed with bone cancer. She was incredibly brave during her treatment and readily agreed to several experimental procedures and tests so as to advance the knowledge of Dr Webster and his team. She trusted him enormously and he was well deserving of her appreciation of him. He took so much time to answer the myriad of questions that came his way. When Dr Webster was not available we got to meet Dr Kirby, a wonderful Christian man who ministered as much to our spiritual needs as well as to Marilyn's physical needs. How blessed we were to receive such fine medical ministry.

The time came for me to take Marilyn to the Heath Hospital for further treatment. On the journey she told me that her time was coming to an end. I tried to change the subject but she would have none of it. She said she had been praying for me and she had been asking the Lord not to leave me on my own for very long. She even suggested a person to me as someone whom she would approve when it came time for me to be married again. At that point I said that I did not want to hear any more. The last part of the journey was spent in silence. When we got to the hospital and Marilyn lay in her bed, I realised I was more interested in protecting myself than in listening to what she had wanted to say, so we continued the conversation. I apologised to her and said that to be speaking about a time when she would not be there was unbearably difficult for me and that I had been selfish and was only considering my situation and not hers. She held my hand and clutching it firmly she told me to listen to her and not to interrupt. Her voice was both calm and strong. She poured out the certainty of her faith and told me what her private prayers had been for the past few months. I felt her faith was putting mine to shame. I was stubbornly continuing to pray for her healing and felt that if I stopped then I would be letting her down. To have interrupted her as she spoke would have been a violation of a most precious moment in time. It was a privilege to hear her speak of what the Lord had told her. She was at peace in her spirit.

Several days later, Marilyn rang me in the evening asking me to come back to the hospital. I feared the worst and drove at a ridiculous speed to get there as soon as I could. When I got to the ward, she thanked me for getting there so soon as there was a man in the bed next to her who needed prayer. Apparently he had brain cancer and had had several procedures to relieve the pressure on his brain from a build-up of cranial fluid. He was scheduled for surgery the following morning. Marilyn had been speaking to him and sharing her faith. She asked him if I could come and pray for him and he had accepted. On the one hand I was incredibly relieved that my worst fears had proved to be unfounded and on the other hand I was stunned that in her moments of great personal need she could be testifying to the man in the bed next to her. Stunned is perhaps the wrong word, because I was in fact proud of her and so impressed with the sheer quality of her character and faith. Many times she had said to me 'suffering either makes you better or bitter'. I was yet again witnessing to the truth of what suffering was doing to Marilyn. It always made her a better person and she was never touched by any tinge of bitterness.

She asked me to lead the prayers for her new friend. I anointed him with Holy Oil and laid hands on his head. I commanded the cancer to leave him and for the peace of God to come over him and give him rest. The following day he went down for his surgery and Marilyn was transferred to the Velindre Hospital.

It was not until fourteen years later that I found out what had happened to the man whom Marilyn befriended. I was taking a Service of Healing at a church in Cardiff and during the time for personal ministry a lady came to the altar rail. I asked her what I should pray for. She asked me if I would forgive her. I asked her what it was she had done that needed forgiveness. She said I had not understood her and that it was she who needed forgiveness from me personally. I confessed I had never met her to my knowledge and was at a loss to understand her request. She asked me if I could remember visiting the Heath Hospital and praying for a man who had brain cancer. I said that I could and she went on to say it was her husband. When he went down for surgery, the doctors could find no trace of cancer in his brain at all. A little while later he was discharged with a clean bill of health. The couple had forgotten all about me during the fourteen years that had elapsed and were passing the church where I was ministering when they noticed the billboard with my name on it. It was then they recalled my name and they hastily agreed to interrupt their journey and go into the church to let me know what had happened at the hospital. She pointed out her husband sitting in the congregation and he was a picture of health. She insisted that I forgive her for not making any effort to let me know the outcome of her husband's surgery. Apparently they were so elated at the news that they completely forgot to try and find out my details to let me know what had happened and express their thanks.

A short while after this incident at the Heath Hospital, Marilyn's condition deteriorated rapidly and unexpectedly. I was with her at the time and within half an hour the Lord took her to Himself. The doctor and nurses said that this should not be happening and could not understand why she was dying. Although she was very ill, she was expected to live for quite a while longer.

I was asked by the staff if I wanted my daughters to come to the hospital. Everything seemed to be happening so quickly. A hasty phone call was made and friends brought Sarah and Emma as quickly as they could. However, Marilyn passed away just minutes before they arrived. Shock, tears, anger, and sheer disbelief combined in a vortex of emotions that carried us down to the depths of loss and lostness.

Marilyn had been right all along. She did live until the children had grown up. Sarah was eighteen and Emma was sixteen. The fact that Marilyn had been such a wonderful wife and mother made the feelings of loss even more intense. There are times when it is incredibly difficult to keep a right focus as a Christian and this without doubt was one of them. I didn't doubt my faith but I was angry with God and I let him know it with great vigour. I didn't even know if I wanted to continue as a priest. All I wanted was to be left alone with my daughters and attempt the impossible task of being a father and a mother to them. The next time I went into Christchurch it was to be on my own. I needed to have it out with God, but as I walked towards the altar, I fell to my knees in tears and then prostrated myself on the carpet as I sensed the awesome presence of God. Instead of expressing my anger and disappointment, I found myself rededicating myself to Him and telling Him I would continue to believe that He does heal today and would wait until I was taken to be reunited with Marilyn in heaven to be told why the Lord had taken her to Himself and not healed her. I asked for a further anointing to be used by Him; to be able to stand firm and to declare in word and deed the truth that God heals and saves today.

21

Totally Blown Away by the Lord's Timing

Just a few weeks after the Lord took Marilyn to be with Him in heaven, our friends John and Alison had an astounding experience. In the early hours of one morning, Alison was awoken as she heard the words, "Steve must go to college". She had never had such an experience before and was stunned by it. She noticed the time on the clock and then went back to sleep. The following night she had the same experience again. She heard the same words and it was at the same time as the previous night. She woke up John and told him the Lord had spoken to her and told her I must go to college. They wondered what this could possibly mean and what should they do about it.

Before I continue the story, I need to digress and tell you a little about the time when both of our families went to France on holiday together. I had decided to run the London Marathon so as to raise funds for the Velindre Hospital in Cardiff as a gesture of thanks for the great care and treatment that they provided for Marilyn during her illness. So whilst on holiday at the campsite there was a great opportunity for some good weather training. One day I asked John if he would hire four bicycles for himself, his daughter Faith and my daughters Sarah and Emma. I chose a circular route and estimated the time that it would take me. They gave me a good head start and we were to see who could get back to the campsite first.

John was a little delayed in setting off as he had difficulty in hiring the bicycle. He did what many Brits abroad do when in a foreign country and are unable to speak the language. He embraced the time-honoured British tradition of speaking English very slowly with a pseudo-French accent whilst using sign language. When that failed, he resorted to plan B which is guaranteed to succeed. He upped his volume control to maximum. The girls said that the picture on the face of the Frenchman was a sight to behold as he took John's money and handed over the bicycles.

All was going well from their point of view as they overtook me about a hundred yards from the last roundabout before the campsite. I could hear John telling the children to keep close to him and to set off around the roundabout when he thought it was safe. John then shouted, "Go!" Another 'Wallbank' moment then hit the poor unsuspecting motorists. The girls all set off nicely and were calmly going around the roundabout. John was way behind them with his bicycle stuck in first gear. He was doing an impression of Sir Chris Hoy, the Olympic cycling champion. His legs were pumping furiously as he crouched over the handlebars whilst reaching a maximum speed of over two miles per hour in a zig zag fashion. Needless to say, the motorists proved themselves to be very supportive of John's valiant efforts and they showed their appreciation by sounding their horns. This only served to spur John on all the more and his legs could only be seen as a blur to the naked eye. The girls and I had met up and were waiting for John to arrive. Around he came with beads of perspiration flying in every direction until he gracefully collapsed on the grass beside us. The passing motorists again showed their appreciation of his efforts by continuing the sounding of their horns and universally recognisable hand gestures accompanied by continental expletives that did not give rise to an easy translation. The suggestion that John should throw a bucket of water over the glowing bicycle chain before he handed his bicycle back fell upon deaf ears!

John and Alison had persuaded myself, Sarah and Emma to go on holiday with them as we were still struggling to come to terms with Marilyn's death. It was a really therapeutic time and we laughed so many times at the ridiculous things that happened. We drove to St Jean de Monts in the Vendee to a large campsite at Bois Masson that had over eight hundred emplacements and took it in turns to lead the way as we drove through France. However, travelling through Rouen we were somewhat alarmed to see the maps flying through the sunroof of John's car in front. Apparently they had had a slight disagreement as to the route they should take and so Alison launched the maps through the sunroof and advised John it would be best if he chose the route himself as he had clearly decided to not avail himself of her map reading skills. In spite of this severe impediment, we eventually got to the campsite in one piece.

The weather was glorious and the facilities were superb. After unpacking, we all wanted to have a barbecue to get the holiday off to a good start. We had a good selection of meats accompanied by the statutory French baguette and salads. The bottles of Muscadet were evaporating rather quickly in the heat of the balmy night when John decided to go into the tent for something. He didn't make it. He had rigged the awning light so that it would give us light outside. As he was about to enter the awning, he garroted himself on the lead of the light and in a millisecond every single light in the whole campsite went out. We were about to dissolve in laughter when a cacophony of noise rose from the hundreds of families who were suddenly plunged into darkness. We thought it might not be wise to own up and joined harmoniously in the cacophony with shouts of, "What's happened? Who put the lights out?" The campsite soon became filled with beams of torchlight accompanied by expletives as people floundered and fumbled about. Eventually the noise died down as families resigned themselves to going to bed early. The following morning there was a flurry of activity as disgruntled campers demanded to know what had caused the electricity to fail the previous evening. Once again we thought that this was a classic situation in which discretion was the better part of valour – so we did not own up. We bought a replacement bulb that day and set off for the beach and the sun. However, that same evening John managed to repeat the incident and once again the whole campsite descended into darkness. I felt really sorry for the campsite employees as they were confronted with a vociferous horde of angry campers the following morning. Poor John was as mortified as he was embarrassed, but the dye was cast and such incidents were by now a feature of what one could expect when in his presence.

As John and Alison considered the 'word' that the Lord had given to Alison, they decided if I was to go to college, then all they could think of was that both John and I really wanted to learn to speak

French. So John came to see me and asked me if I would like to go with him to a Leisure French course that was to start soon in the local college. However, he failed to tell me what the Lord had given to Alison and I sent him away with a flea in his ear as I considered the invitation to be both inappropriate and insensitive so soon after our family bereavement. Not to be outdone, John then went to the college and paid the subscription fee for both of us. He returned and presented me with news of what he had done. I very reluctantly agreed to go with him.

When we arrived at the college for the first night of the course, there were far too many people to form a single class and so we were divided into two groups. The groups were to be those who were total beginners and those who had a smattering of French. I said that I could speak 'schoolboy' French but that my biggest difficulty was that whenever I visited France I could never find a schoolboy to speak to! This didn't go down too well with the teacher but served to set the tone for what followed during the course.

I had decided I would use the course as a distraction therapy from the pains of bereavement and not take it at all seriously. I played the part of the class idiot – a role that came quite naturally to me. I was always doing something to make the class laugh during the lessons. We followed our text book, *A Vous La France*, diligently, so I knew what would be taught at the next lesson. When it came to the chapter on restaurants and food, I took to the class a clove of garlic and some freshly ground coffee. During the lesson I rubbed the garlic on the underside of the desk and sprinkled some of the coffee on the floor. One of the elderly pupils then exclaimed it was remarkable, that as the lesson was progressing, she could not only imagine being in a restaurant but it actually smelt as if she was in one. This prompted other students to say they too were having the same experience. The teacher knew full well who was causing a distraction but simply ignored me and carried on with the lesson. However, the *'coup de gras'* happened when I arrived late one evening as a result of being at a service in a local church. I entered the class over an hour late wearing my clerical garb. The teacher took one look at me and told me to get on with it so she could continue. Little did we know she had been to a function the previous week in which a Strippergram appeared much to the riotous amusement of all who were there.

When the teacher told me to get on with it, I did not know what she meant. The class cottoned on before I did, and then one of them said to the teacher that I was a real vicar and not a Strippergram. The class felt sorry for Sian, but at the same time, try as they might, they could not control their laughter. I was truly impressed with Sian's reaction. She seemed to take it all in her stride and promptly got on with the lesson. I have to admit attending those French lessons was extremely therapeutic for me and I was thankful to John for insisting I went with him. However, at that time he had still not told me of the 'word' the Lord had given to Alison. The first term finished in December and I was not looking forward to Christmas at all.

A significant change happened in my prayer life after I had rededicated myself to the Lord following the great sense of loss when the Lord took Marilyn to Himself. I had asked the Lord to lead me into a deeper relationship with Him. Then, one day, during my prayer time I felt the Lord saying to me that I would have to pray for eight hours every day. I was confounded and confused yet again. Surely this could not have come from the Lord? But it seemed so clear. So I asked Him to let me know how this could be done. I sensed Him say after I had finished my last prayers at night I was to ask Him to consecrate my sleep as a time of communion with Him in which He would do all the talking and I was to take care not to say 'Amen' until I woke in the morning. I did this, and my final prayer at night went like this. "Lord I pray that my bed might be like an operating table; you are the surgeon; I sign my name on the dotted line and give my consent for whatever you want to do in my life this night".

From that time onwards I have kept a pen and paper close at hand so that when I awake in the night with a revelation or insight, then I could write it down. My dream life took on a new dimension. There were times when I would see and 'hear' what Jesus was saying to people I knew. The following day I would arrange to meet them and either through conversation or prayer share what I believed I had been given by the Lord for them.

Now the reason for writing this at this stage of my story was that on the night before the last lesson of the first term, I had a dream about Sian in which the Lord was holding her in His arms. She was very tearful and being comforted. I woke up and started to receive Words of Knowledge with regards to what was making Sian so tearful. I quickly grabbed my notebook and pen and started to write down all I was being given. The detail of the incidents of brokenness and sadness was something I had never experienced before. In the past I had only received a sentence or two of Words of Knowledge, but these Words of Knowledge seemed to be going on forever.

In the morning, I went to the study and typed out all I had been given. It came to four sheets of A4 paper. I asked the Lord what I was to do with all this very personal information and I sensed He wanted me to give it to her. So I put the four pages in an envelope and gave it to her at the end of the lesson that night. I told her I had been in prayer for her and if any of the contents in the envelope were accurate then I would be glad to spend some time with her to talk and pray about them. She thanked me and the conversation ended rather abruptly. Then, the Sunday before Christmas I woke up with words in my mind, 'Pray for Sian'. I sat up in bed and was startled by my reaction because I said I wouldn't do it. I paused for a moment to consider what was an instinctive reaction and felt a great sense of nervousness without knowing why. The words 'pray for Sian' were still in my mind and I continued to protest I would not do it. So I put the light on in the bedroom and started to read my bible. Surely God would not interfere if I was reading the bible? How amazingly misguided of me to think such a thing. The words 'pray for Sian' continued to impress themselves upon my mind.

At this point in time I started to feel something of an adrenaline rush as my nervousness increased. I got out of bed and went downstairs to make a pot of coffee whilst resolving if I was to stay up all night I would still not pray for Sian. The hours went by and at six o'clock I finally gave in. I confessed my fear and said I was sorry for resisting but I was sensing in my spirit that the request to pray for Sian was more than I felt I could handle. Then I asked the Lord what it was He wanted me to pray for. In an instant the words came into my mind, 'Pray for Sian to be your wife'. I shot up from the study chair and shouted to the Lord that he couldn't be serious. It was only a matter of weeks since Marilyn had passed away. It just didn't make any sense to me and as I sat down again in the chair I cupped my hands and held my head and burst into tears. I don't have any words to describe what I was feeling. Just like the emotional pains of bereavement stand alone as being incomparable with anything else, so what I was feeling felt like no other emotion I had ever experienced. No words could accompany this startling new emotion and there was no way I could pray. My first service was at eight o'clock that morning so I had to get ready for it. In a sense I was glad to have a reason to step back from this experience and focus my attention on all that would be needed for the Sunday services.

The first Christmas without Marilyn was very difficult. Emotions were still raw and the joy of Christmastime seemed irreconcilable to the sense of loss that flowed in waves over Sarah, Emma and myself. The tiniest of things seemed to set us off and reduce us to tears such as a glance at a photograph, something that Marilyn had bought for us, or something that we now had to do because she was no longer there. Marilyn had been a truly amazing mother and wife. She had always said that nothing gave her more happiness than being a mother as it was the greatest occupation that any woman could ever have. Her favourite saying 'suffering either makes you better or bitter' became very poignant for each of us in the weeks after Marilyn's death. Marilyn told me many times she had prayed that Sarah and Emma would not lose their faith when it came time for the Lord to take her. She knew her passing would be a great blow to their faith and that it would take quite some time for them to recover. She was right – we were angry with God, we were dismayed and shocked at the suddenness of Marilyn's leaving. We went to the cemetery at Abercynon where Marilyn's ashes were buried. It was her wish to be laid to rest close to the grave of her parents who had lived there for many years. As we laid the flowers down we just held each other and wept together. The inevitable question 'why' was cried out as we were truly lost in the mystery of the will of God.

A few days after Christmas, Sian contacted me to affirm the Words of Knowledge that I had given to her, and asked to see me so she could receive Prayer Ministry. She came to the vicarage shortly afterwards and I explained to her what Prayer Ministry was and what it would involve. She told me her faith story and how she had been a regular attender at an international Baptist Church in Geneva. In her late teens, she had been identified and singled out as an exceptionally talented player of the bassoon. Arrangements were made for her to go to Freiburg in Germany to complete her education and at the same time to study music as a bassoonist. From Germany she went to

Switzerland where she joined the *Swisse Ramonde National Orchestra*. She was enjoying a wonderful career and had been touring with the orchestra to many parts of the world until her mother became ill with cancer. Sian relinquished her position in the orchestra in order to come home and nurse her. When her mother passed away, she was invited by Dilwyn, a senior manager at Merthyr Technical College, to teach a Leisure French class. I had known Dilwyn for many years as he was a lecturer at the college when I taught a Social and Life Skills course there in the late 1970s. I had had a number of discussions about the Christian Faith with Dilwyn as he was a Non-Conformist church leader and preacher. This lovely Christian man was the instrument the Lord used to bring Sian to the college for she and I eventually to meet.

It was just a few weeks into the Spring Term of the French course when Sian dropped a bombshell to the class. She told us she was not going to be able to complete the course with us as she had received an offer of employment with François Léotard, the French Foreign Minister. It was then she told us for the first time when she was living in Geneva she taught English as a foreign language to diplomats at the United Nations. She was fluent in German and French, and when the orchestra was not on tour she had the time to teach English at the United Nations. The class was stunned by her news that she would be leaving as she got on so well with everybody and was much liked. Her style of teaching meant she was quite strict about homework being done and paying attention, but also embraced lighter moments of humour. I was totally thrown by the news of her departure and found it difficult to concentrate on the remainder of the lesson. In my mind I kept on asking the Lord what on earth was I to do?

I didn't receive any response from the Lord and went home after the lesson quite bemused. Sensing that an act of faith was what was needed, I rang the Booking Office at St David's Hall in Cardiff and booked two tickets for the concert on the Saturday after Sian said she would be leaving. I also made a reservation for an evening meal after the concert. I know this was very disrespectful, but when I put the phone down, I said to the Lord this was my faith reaction to the news of Sian's departure and He could stuff it in His pipe and smoke it. I told Him that the ball was in His court now and I would not do anything or say anything to Sian in the meantime. It was His move.

Now I was really going to find out if He really wanted us to get married or not.

The weeks went by and we were getting close to the date when Sian said she would be taking up her new appointment in Paris. Then, at the start of a lesson, she announced to the class she had felt uneasy in her spirit about the situation concerning the appointment and she had declined the offer and would be able to complete the French Course at the college. My heart was in my mouth. All the emotions of affection for Sian that I had been holding back just gushed out. I felt an overwhelming love for her and knew without a doubt we would be married. After the lesson had been completed, I asked if I could speak to her. When everyone had left I asked if she would like to come with me to the concert at St David's Hall and have a meal together afterwards. I thought it best not to tell her that I already had the tickets and the meal reservation. To do so might have seemed just a little presumptuous or perhaps more accurately, utter lunacy.

Our first date wasn't the best by any stretch of the imagination. Sian thought the orchestra was rather poor and the meal we had was nothing to write home about. However, our relationship had begun and we continued dating each other. Sian took a job with a company that provided teaching English as a foreign language to international students from a variety of businesses. At the end of her working week, I would go to her house and make a meal for her. Let me say at this point we were still learning a lot about each other every time we met. I say this as a lame excuse for what happened next.

It was on a Friday night and I was at her home preparing an evening meal when the telephone rang. I picked up the telephone and on the line was someone with a thick French accent. He said he was in London and wanted Sian to go to London to help him to prepare a speech. I thought it was someone fooling around so I asked him who he was. When he told me his name I told him to cut out the funny stuff and tell me who he really was. He became agitated and demanded to know who I was. I told him that I was Sian's boyfriend. He was clearly not impressed at all by me and repeated the request for Sian to visit him at his hotel in London. I asked him again who he was, but he simply repeated the same ridiculous name that he had given me before. I asked him one more time to let me know who he really was and he promptly put the phone down on me. When Sian got home, I told her I had had a strange phone call from a wind up merchant who used a thick French accent. She asked if he gave a name. I told her the name he gave me and she let out a loud gasp of, "Oh no!" I asked what the matter was and she then told me I had spoken to the President of France, Jacques Chirac. Poor Sian was absolutely horrified. What a blunder! What an absolute blunder! I felt a prize prat of the first order. Sian then rang dear, poor confused 'Jacques' and apologised profusely telling him she had a new boyfriend who knew precious little about her yet. Oh if only the ground could have swallowed me up. As I stood waiting for a tirade from Sian I noticed a grin beginning to appear and much to my relief it progressed into laughter. It was at this point I realised that not even my worst gaffs were going got put her off. Praise the Lord!

It obviously came as quite a shock to the congregation when Sian first appeared on the scene. This was entirely understandable so soon after Marilyn's passing. And it did make for some awkward moments that Sian found especially difficult. Merthyr Tydfil is made up of very close knit communities and the jungle drums beat louder when a stranger appears in their midst. Someone once put it like this, "It's not that we are nosey, but we have a healthy interest other people's business." The trouble was that no one knew Sian or her family or her history. Fortunately I had a number of close friends in the parish and they made Sian feel welcome and loved. It would be wrong to give the impression that the congregation were in any way hostile to Sian and it wasn't very long before they showed her what a strong Christian family we were.

Sian and I became engaged at Easter time in 1991 and we made an appointment to see Bishop Roy Davies to tell him our news. He was perfectly charming towards Sian and after reaching for his diary, he told us he could conduct the wedding in October. Sian and I hadn't even spoken about setting a date or who we might like to take our wedding. When we told this to Bishop Roy, he wasn't at all put off, neither was he to be dissuaded. When we left, he had given us the date and told us he would be in touch later to make the arrangements. We were quite taken aback as it all seemed to be so rushed. It didn't seem as if we had any say in the timing of our coming together, the Lord saw to that, and now we didn't seem to have any say in the choosing of our wedding day, Bishop Roy had seen to that.

22

A Stag Night That Hit the National Press

For my stag night some of the men in the Church and I hired the Llandow Go-Karting Track and we organised a competition between ourselves. It was fiercely competitive and great fun except for the fact we managed to write off two Go-Karts. It was a strange thing to see what a Go-Kart can do to normal level-headed Christians. It was as if the protective suits and helmets covered every ounce of Christianity in them and left them to the mercy of every conceivable road rage behaviour. No quarter was given, much to the chagrin of the Go-Karting staff who abortively tried to encourage sanity and safety. The manager asked me during one of the breaks if I was the vicar. When I said that I was, he asked if I had any control whatsoever over the bunch of madmen who were creating mayhem on the track. But by that time it was far too late. It was with a huge sigh of relief that the competition ended.

After the racing we went to a local hostelry where we had booked a meal. All was going well when a policeman, who was supposed to be a friend, decided to put me in handcuffs. Oh Yes! This was great fun wasn't it? It seemed harmless enough until they hatched a plot to take me back to Merthyr Tydfil town centre and handcuff me to a lamp post minus my trousers. I knew they were serious and the more I protested that enough was enough, the more elaborate became their plans. I simply had to escape or I would never be able to live it down if their plan succeeded. So I hatched a plot. One of my friends, Lyn, who had arrived in his car was my accomplice. I said I needed to go the toilet. When I got there, I climbed onto one of the washbasins, opened the window above it and jumped out. My friend then hid me in the back of his car. He said he had to leave early and drove slowly out of the car park so as not to draw attention to himself. When the rest of the men discovered that I was missing, they panicked. They thought I had jumped out of the window and was hiding nearby. They searched everywhere they could think I might be hiding to no avail. They went into people's gardens, looked in ditches and fields. They were terrified to go back to Merthyr Tydfil without me, but in the end they gave up and thought I was lost. By now it was way past midnight. One of the party was delegated to return to the vicarage where Sian was having a small party of her own with my daughters Sarah and Emma, together with Alison Wallbank and Marie Williams.

Meanwhile, Lyn had brought me back to the vicarage. There was only one slight problem. I still had the handcuffs on. With great dexterity, Marie decided to use a hair clip to get the handcuffs off. Her son was the one who put the handcuffs on in the first place. However, it soon became obvious he had miserably failed to show his mother how to use a hair clip to unlock handcuffs. The handcuffs became tighter and tighter until my fingers started to turn to a dark police blue. I told her to give up and I was going to ring the local police station and ask for help.

Well, you can just imagine the conversation I had with the sergeant at the desk when I told him that I was the vicar of Cyfarthfa Church and I was in handcuffs. Eventually I managed to persuade him that I was who I claimed to be. He said he would send a squad car to the vicarage and the officers would use their keys to try to extricate me from my predicament. A squad car arrived within a matter of minutes and four officers came to the door. None of their keys would fit so they said they would have to take me to the nearby Fire Station to have the handcuffs cut off. One of the kind officers asked if I wanted a blanket. I thanked him very much for his consideration and replied I did not as it was not very cold. He then retorted that it was not to keep the cold out, but to hide who I was so that nobody would be able to see me. We all laughed and I duly walked out without the blanket, handcuffed, with the four police officers. It was in the early hours of the morning and just as I was about to get into the police car, two cars passed by very slowly as the occupants took a good look at what was happening.

Now, the Fire Station was opposite a well frequented night club. Just as we arrived at the Fire Station the night club was disgorging itself of the night's revellers. With that, a loud shout came from amongst the crowd, "Look boys, it's the vicar!" Instead of minding their own business and making their way to their homes, they gathered to watch the side show I was putting on. A fireman used a metal cutter to get the handcuffs off, to the great applause of the onlookers. Why oh why did I not agree to the use of a blanket? As if things weren't as bad as they were already, my embarrassment was compounded further. One of the men on my stag night, Robert, was the husband of a well-known BBC reporter Melanie Doel. The couple were also in the Leisure French class that Sian taught in the local college. It was inevitable that Melanie would soon get the story. The article appeared in all the local press as well as the *London Evening Standard* and a Liverpool newspaper. I am glad that I decided to confess to Bishop Roy what had happened because on the day that Sian and I were married, members of the Press arrived to take our photographs and somewhat embellish the story. One of the photographers had the audacity to bring a pair of handcuffs and asked Sian if she would put them on me. He thought it would be a fitting photograph to go with the caption, "Holy Wedlock?" She declined in a tone of voice that left him in no doubt that his equipment was being put in extreme jeopardy. In the meantime, Bishop Roy discretely hid himself from view.

Healing, Heartache and Humour

23

Another Episcopal Visit to the Parish

Bishop Ephraim, from Nigeria, came to visit the Diocese and spent a few days in our parish staying with Jim and Margaret. It was a lovely sunny day when I picked him up from the train station and took him to their home. When we arrived, Jim was in the garden wearing a knotted handkerchief, old shirt, long khaki shorts, short socks and black shoes. As soon as the Bishop saw Jim he said that he had wanted to meet him for a very long time. Jim felt a little embarrassed and was in the process of ingratiating himself when the Bishop said, "Doctor Livingstone, I presume". That set the tone of the visit and humour played a great part for the remainder of his time with us. By the time he left he was armed with scores of jokes, most of them Irish, which Jim had shared with him.

A collection was made for the Bishop and he wanted to buy clothes to take home with him. My wife Sian was delegated to take him to Makro buy the clothes. When Sian asked him what he wanted to buy, he said he would like some suits. A young lady assistant introduced herself and asked how she could assist him. When he said that he wanted suits, she got out her tape measure to measure the Bishop. He caught hold of the tape and asked her if she was married. When she replied in the negative, he took the tape from her and promptly gave it to Sian saying that she could measure him – inside leg and all. After this ordeal, Sian breathed a sigh of relief and thinking that her embarrassment was over, asked what he would like to purchase with the money that was remaining. The Bishop replied that he would like to buy some special underwear for his wife. Sian paused nervously before tentatively asking him what exactly he meant by special underwear. Bishop Ephraim said that he would like some silk underwear for his wife. Then came the fateful question. "What size is she?" said Sian, to which the Bishop replied, cupping his hands in front of his chest, "About this size". At this, Sian and the assistant nearly lost it altogether. When Sian returned home, she made me promise that never again would I send her to go shopping with an African Bishop as she nearly died of embarrassment. In fact, she has never been to Makro since!

24

Meeting John Wimber

I was greatly impacted by the ministry of John Wimber when he and his team from the Anaheim Vineyard Christian Fellowship in California came to lead a conference at Westminster Central Hall in London in 1984. Shortly afterwards, I read his book *Signs and Wonders and Church Growth* and I just knew in my spirit I wanted to go on a journey of discovery to learn so much more about the power of the Kingdom of God and the implications this could have on my life and ministry. So when John Wimber accepted an invitation in 1994 to conduct a conference in the City Temple, Cardiff, I quickly signed up for it together with several of my church leaders. Testimonies of what we saw and heard were hugely influential in confirming belief that we were privileged to be living in a Christian era in which the Church was rediscovering the gifts and ministries of the Holy Spirit especially the ministry of healing.

On another occasion, Rev Geoff Waggett and I had a private meeting with John Wimber at the Angel Hotel in Cardiff. As we sat down, the thought came to my mind he looked like a Father Christmas figure with his white hair and beard. Then into my spirit came the words, 'he has gifts to bring, listen to him'. Geoff and I had a number of things we wanted to say to him and questions to ask him, but we barely touched on our agenda. We listened as he spoke to us. His words of encouragement and insight were profound indeed and we left having been greatly blessed. The impact upon me was like an endorsement for the spiritual path I was taking and an encouragement to press on in spite of personal mistakes, setbacks and disappointments.

Bishop David Pytches, the vicar of St Andrew's in Chorleywood was also greatly influenced by John Wimber. David was the founder of New Wine conferences and hosted retreats in his parish for church leaders. These retreats included times for personal ministry for each participant and when the Rev John Parkin attended, he received a prophetic word that he was being called to 'build a church within a church'. At the time, this meant nothing to John but he kept it in his heart as he was sure that it was from the Lord. Several years before this, as I was prayerfully considering what kind of ministry would be effective in a local council estate, I sensed the Lord telling me that he would provide a dedicated priest to work on the estate. I told the good news of this revelation to the small congregation we had at St Luke's church on the estate. They asked the obvious questions such as how could we afford a curate even if we were granted permission to have one, and where would he live. It was probably not surprising they did not take me seriously. Since the time that I had been the vicar, St Luke's had not experienced any growth and I was at a loss to know what to do next. I made enquiries at the time as to the possibility of having a curate and had a very negative response. In truth, I genuinely felt I had made a mistake and not heard rightly from the Lord. However, a few years later, during a time of prayer the Rev John Parkin came to mind.

I sensed the Lord encouraging me to ask John if he was interested in building a church within a church. When I telephoned John, he told me when he went on a retreat for church leaders at St Andrew's, Chorleywood, he received exactly the same words in a prophecy given to him. We duly contacted the Bishop and within a short period of time John was appointed as a Priest Missioner dedicated to work on the Gellideg Estate. The diocese paid him a full vicar's salary and he and his wife Angie came to live on the estate. Some members of Christchurch were commissioned to form the basis of a church plant that would evangelise the estate under John's leadership.

I had made the mistake of trying to push the outworking of the initial word I had received from the Lord immediately after receiving it. This is why I became discouraged and doubted if the prophetic word had indeed come from the Lord. I needed to wait for the Lord's timing and not be discouraged. If the prophetic word came from the Lord then it would definitely come about, but if it was from my inner longing then nothing would happen. Only time would tell. It was a good lesson to learn.

Robin S. Sharma, the Canadian writer and speaker, once said, "The mind is a wonderful servant, but a terrible master". I often struggle with the application of this truth. When I hear of someone being ill or in great need, my instinctive reaction is to want to be with them. However, I am slowly learning to pray, before I set off to visit the person in distress, and ask the Lord what it is He wants me to pray or say.

On Wednesday, January 28th 1998, I had a telephone call to let me know that a very prominent Christian man in Merthyr Tydfil was gravely ill in hospital.

David was a leader in the Full Gospel Businessman's Fellowship. He was a regular speaker at their events and loved to sing gospel songs with a voice that truly plucked at the heart strings. When I asked the Lord what I should pray, instead of receiving a word for healing or encouragement, I felt a firm conviction not to see him. This confused me greatly and I pleaded with the Lord let me see him – to no avail. I continued to pray for David in my prayer times and on Monday 2nd February the Lord finally gave me a word for him. David wrote these words in a letter that he sent to me years later, "It was while you were in your kitchen that He spoke to you, 'Go and tell David that I will do for him what I did for Hezekiah.' I know the story well. What a word! I've told countless people that story and that's why I wouldn't buy a mobile phone, as some suggested I did, because I began to walk alone in the countryside. To have a mobile phone would most definitely have been a belt and braces job. If God's Word didn't work, well there's the mobile phone to call someone. It's now 16 years, the day before yesterday. Praise God. What a Saviour!"

David is now with his Lord in glory having brought many to salvation and healing through his impressive prayer life.

On another occasion when I was visiting a church member in Prince Charles Hospital, I recognised a priest colleague of mine in a single bed unit. Robert was a vicar from a nearby parish. He told me he had just received the bad news he had a condition called lupus and that the condition was so advanced there was no hope of recovery. He was advised to settle all his affairs when he returned home. After we spoke for a while, the time came for me to anoint him and pray for his healing. I cannot say I experienced any great surge of faith when I prayed for him. Afterwards, Robert thanked me and as he did so I noticed the look in his eyes. If the eyes are the window to the soul, then Robert's eyes were filled with faith and love. As I left him, it came to me that the faith for his healing came more from him than from me.

Several weeks later, Robert came to see me with the story of his healing. He had been to see his local doctor and the doctor told him that he did not believe he had lupus. Further tests were done and they confirmed the condition was no longer there. To say he was delighted would be an understatement. He had a new lease of life. However, it did not seem to be very long before he became ill again. This time it was a result of receiving metal poisoning as a child. Once again he was told nothing could be done and the consequences would remain permanent. Once again, he was totally healed after a time of prayer. On a third occasion he asked me to call at his vicarage to pray for him as he had a throat condition that did not respond to medical treatment. Once more, after a time of prayer, he was completely healed.

I give this instance as an encouragement to those who have been healed through prayer and who subsequently become ill again. Some feel that it is an imposition to ask again for prayer for healing. There is nothing further from the truth than this. It is always the will of God to answer prayer. The answer may not be the answer that we want or in the time that we want, but God's love is a constant. *"Cast all your anxieties upon him because he cares for you,"* (1 Peter 5:6).

25

From the Golf Course to Hospital

When my knees began to show signs of wear and tear, I gave up running and took up golf. Morlais Castle Golf Course was only four miles away and once again I was able to enjoy fresh air and exercise. Huw, the Professional at the club, was a Christian and he taught me how to pray and play my way around the course. I somehow managed to get my handicap down to 14 and in the year that I won a competition at the club, I also won the Church in Wales Clergy Golf Championship at Llangollen. The following year in 2000 saw the establishment of a competition named the Cranmer Cup in which Anglican clergy from Great Britain and Ireland took on their counterparts in America.

The Ryder Cup-type format proved a great success. I played in the first competition at the George T. Bagby State Park in Georgia. Prior to the event, the American captain sent several emails to us about the conditions at the Park. The first email apologised for the fact that the event was going to be held during the snake mating season. However, he kindly reassured us there was a glass fronted refrigerator in the Club House that contained syringes of antidote for all the local snakes. Above each syringe was a photograph of a snake. If anyone was bitten, we were instructed to be rushed to the Club House in the golf buggies provided, identify the offending snake from the photographs and be injected with the antidote. This was extremely helpful for all but the colour blind players, and I was one of them. I jokingly said to the administrator if I was brought in as a victim, then he should give me every single injection as there was no way I could identify the coloured markings of the offending snake.

Our captain trod on a Water Moccasin snake when looking for his ball in the rough, he fell over and was hurriedly dragged back onto the fairway before the snake bit him. His game never recovered and he had nightmares each evening. The only snakes that I saw were mating in a bunker when an eagle came swooping down and flew off with the deal of the day – two for the price of one.

A second email arrived to say there were alligators on all the holes that had a water hazard. Once again, we were given very helpful instructions as to what to do if one was unfortunate enough to be chased by such a beast. Apparently, if one runs away in a zig zag direction, then the chasing monster gives up quickly as it loses its balance in its inner ear.

Subsequent events revealed that not all of the American contestants had taken heed of this information. On the last hole of the practice round there was an elevated green alongside a large pond. I looked to see if there was an alligator in the pond and could not see one. Then, just as an American was walking backwards towards the pond, eyeing up his putt, I saw an alligator on the bank with its nose level with the green. It was eyeing up a snap lunch coming towards it. I shouted, "Alligator, run!" With that, the American threw his putter into the air, screamed at the top of his voice with a rich variety of expletives that could never be put into print and ran IN A STRAIGHT LINE as fast as his legs could propel him.

Two years later, the Cranmer Cup was held at the Hallamshire Golf Club in Sheffield. Having won the Church in Wales Championship for a second time, I was selected for the home team in what proved to be my last game of golf for a long time. Whilst walking down a fairway, I put my foot down a rabbit hole and injured my ankle. Two holes later, I couldn't carry on and had to retire. On arriving back home, I went to the local hospital and X-rays revealed that I had three fractures. Shortly afterwards I had a pulmonary embolism and was admitted to hospital. As I lay in bed on the first night, a man was brought into the bed next to me. It was well past midnight and the commotion he made woke up those who were asleep. He was obviously worse the wear for drink. Just as we were settling down to sleep, he shouted out he wanted to go to the toilet. The nurse came and offered him a bedpan but he refused. Within a short time he shouted out another three times and each time he refused a bedpan. On the third occasion the ward sister came with a nurse and after pulling the curtain around his bed she stood him up and told the nurse to tickle him. Riotous laughter broke out when the sister was heard to say, "Not there nurse, there!" No matter where I go, humour seems to lurk close by, just waiting for an opportunity to leap out. However, on this occasion the laughter brought strong chest pains with it and I honestly thought that the Lord was about to take me to Himself. I prayed prayers of repentance and blessings on my family and finished with singing praise songs in my mind. The pains gradually eased and I thanked the Lord for His healing grace.

The following day the Bishop of Llandaff came to see me outside of visiting hours. He blessed each patient in the ward and then began praying for me. There was complete silence in the ward as he anointed me. I really felt that I was being blessed by the Lord as he prayed. No sooner had he left when a police officer arrived. It was Darren. He was the one who handcuffed me on my stag night. As Darren stood at the foot of my bed we were disturbed by the noise of someone falling on the floor. It was the patient at the far end of the ward. When we looked to see where he was, he was hiding under the bed. Apparently he was a man who was wanted by the police and as soon as he saw Darren he got out of bed so quickly that he fell. Later, the same day, I was taken in a wheelchair to pray for Darren's grandfather, Bryn, who had been admitted to the hospital.

Healing, Heartache and Humour

26

People Before Politics

In 2003, the Churches of Merthyr Tydfil had their usual March of Witness during Lent. We would pray outside various locations in the town centre including the Town Hall. Our prayers were for the spiritual and material prosperity of the town. However, on this occasion, when we were praying outside the Town Hall, there was a prophetic word that the Lord wanted the gospel to be preached in the Civic Centre, and even more specifically in the Council Chamber. Although none of us could imagine how on earth this could happen, we prayed with a conviction that took me aback. As we reflected on this later on, it was clear none of us had any access to the Town Hall that could bring this about and we would have to wait and see what the Lord might do at some future time.

Later that year, I was asked if I would like to help in the founding of a new political party with a view to becoming a Councillor for the Local Authority. My heart greatly warmed towards the idea but I tried to shrug it off as I considered the implications of such a radical change for my life and ministry. I interpreted my positive reaction to the invitation to be a fleshly desire and not a response to something the Lord wanted me to do. However, when I committed the situation to prayer, to my surprise, I felt an even greater urge to want to run with it. When I shared the matter with my church leadership there was a very mixed response. Most of the leaders were not convinced this was what the Lord wanted for me and I could entirely understand their reaction. It was a strange emotional tug of war. My heart was racing with the potential of being a Christian witness in a secular environment and yet I was also feeling afraid of what the implications would be for the Church. In the end, my leadership agreed that I could embark on this venture if I gave assurances as to how much time it would take and not neglect my Church responsibilities.

It was agreed the new political party would be named *People Before Politics* and meetings were held in the Church Hall as we gathered candidates for the local elections in 2004. We had 22 candidates and won nine seats at the election. I became the Leader of the Opposition as we had the second highest number of successful candidates. What did I know about local politics? Nothing. What experience did I have of local politics? None. How steep was the learning curve about local politics? Monumental, and I felt like a fish out of water.

I knew with a surety that the Lord had called me into this venture, but I really struggled in this highly charged political environment. What I enjoyed most was the time spent engaging with the officers and being able to pray with them; solving the problems of constituents; helping in the development of strategies for the delivery of Social Services. Then, out of the blue, one day I was asked by an Officer if I would consider establishing a monthly meeting for Christians working for the Local Authority. I readily agreed to this and we had some very encouraging meetings and times of prayer. At one of the meetings, I presented an overview of the *Alpha Course*. This course was promoted worldwide by Holy Trinity Brompton in London through the Rev Nicky Gumbel. Many thousands of people had become Christians as a result of taking part in this course. After my brief presentation, one of the Officers asked if I would be prepared to lead the entire course. I readily agreed to this and arrangements were made for me to lead the course in one of the meeting rooms in the Civic Centre. On the day of the first part of the course, the equipment did not work, so permission was given to use the Council Chamber. Sometimes I am rather slow on the uptake and it was not until I got home that night that I remembered the prophetic word that had been spoken during the Christian March of Witness in the town the previous year. As it turned out, we were able to deliver the entire Alpha Course in the Council Chamber. What had seemed impossible had been made possible by our Lord. Truly, nothing is impossible for Him and it was a time of great blessing for all those involved.

27

The Alpha Course at Christchurch

The use of the *Alpha Course* at Christchurch proved a great success and a number of people became Christians as a result. When we started using it we invited church members to do the course so the church would feel comfortable with this evangelistic resource. It also meant our members could commend the course to their friends and neighbours having done it themselves. The course was packed with impressive illustrations, testimonies and life stories and presented in such a way so as not to leave the participants feeling that they had received a sermon or been in a bible class. Having a meal together before looking at the tapes was extremely important as people could get to know each other socially and then be less inhibited in asking questions after each session.

One of the many highlights was when we organised a national Alpha Conference at a local hotel. Nicky Gumbel and several of his Alpha Team came from Holy Trinity Brompton to promote the use of the *Alpha Course*. Archbishop Rowan Williams attended the conference and was effulgent in his praise for the quality and content of the course.

However, the highlight for me in the delivery of the *Alpha Course* was when Lyn and Malcolm hosted it in their home. The start of the course wasn't particularly auspicious. A lady named Trudy brought her partner Michael. He was not the least bit interested in doing the course and openly said he was only there because Trudy wanted to come. When we started watching one of the tapes, Michael fell asleep and a short while later he started to snore. Trudy nudged him and told him off for embarrassing her and disturbing everyone. Zoe, one of the participants, began to show signs of being in pain. She apologised and said that she could not concentrate on watching the tape as she was experiencing a pain increasing in her back. We stopped the tape and I said that the session on *Does God Heal Today?* was not for another two weeks but we had to speak a little about it and then pray for the healing of her back. As we prayed for her, she felt a sensation of warmth in her spine and within a few minutes the pain eased and then went altogether.

Zoe's daughter was also attending and after she saw what had happened to her mother she asked for prayer. Two Words of Knowledge were given to her as an encouragement both for her and all those present. The first was that she had an accident when she was eight years old and the second was that the accident occurred when she fell off on the right hand side of the horse she was riding. She said there was no way we could have known this information and so we had to give a little background teaching on the Gifts of the Holy Spirit and the gift of knowledge in particular. At this point Michael became extremely attentive and he sat on the edge of his chair.

The consequence of the accident was that one of her legs was shorter than the other. We asked her to sit down, close her eyes, and stretch out her legs until she felt that they were level with each other. Indeed one of her legs was a few inches shorter than the other. We began to pray for the Lord to bring her His healing grace and to cause her leg to grow. Michael's eyes were on stalks as her leg began to grow. It took quite a few minutes for her legs to become the same length and when she got up to walk it took a few moments for her to adjust her balance. The sense of the presence of the Lord in the room was profound indeed and we gave thanks to Him for what we had witnessed. Michael had seen and believed. He was now fully attentive during each session and thoroughly enjoying the course. However, before the course had finished, Michael had an accident in his Karate class and had broken his leg. Malcolm and I visited Michael, and Trudy was at his bedside.

Michael had had surgery and his leg was in plaster. Malcolm and I placed our hands gently on the broken leg and began to pray for the Lord's healing grace to accelerate the natural healing processes. Although my hands were on the plaster cast I could feel movement in the palms of my hands. Turning to Malcolm, I asked him if he sensed anything was happening. He said that he could feel movement in his palms. Realising that the Lord was answering our prayer immediately, I asked Trudy to put her hands on the plaster cast and she also felt there was movement. We thanked the Lord for His healing grace and after a short while we left.

The following day, Michael was taken for an X-ray. When the Consultant came to see Michael he told him the X-ray had revealed weeks of healing had happened overnight and he was at a loss to explain it. Emboldened by this news, he told the consultant about the prayer for healing he had received the previous evening and subsequently spoke to all his fellow patients in the ward. He was not the least deterred by some of the negative reactions he was given. He had a testimony that no-one could take away from him.

Healing, Heartache and Humour

28

New Wine

When Bruce Collins came to live in South Wales in 2007, he initially retained his role on the *New Wine* Leadership Team overseeing the development of *New Wine* in England and abroad. It wasn't very long before he brought his vast experience to bear in the revitalising of *New Wine* in Wales. After travelling the length and breadth of Wales, he gathered a number of leaders together at Llangasty Retreat House near Brecon. I found the time we spent together quite inspirational and my spirit became really excited when I realised what was happening had been prophesied some years earlier.

Two prophecies in particular came to mind. The first was in the early 1970s when I was delegated by the Church in Wales to be a part of a large group to attend a conference held at St Michael Le Belfrey in York. David Watson was the vicar and he shared the story of how his church had grown remarkably in a fairly short period of time and the principles and values that were now embedded in the DNA of the church for continued sustainability and growth. There were so many leaders from Wales at the conference that an additional meeting was held on one of the free evenings. During the worship there were great cries of petition for God to visit Wales again with another revival like the one led by Evan Roberts on 1904. Anne Watson, David's wife, then asked if she could address the assembled leaders. She said she had just received a prophetic word that God was not going to give Wales another revival like the last one. However, she went on to say that God was going to bring revival to Wales, but it was going to be very different compared to previous revivals. There was a very mixed reaction to this prophecy and the meeting became a little subdued as a result. The second prophecy came out of a meeting hosted by the Earl of Powis in Powis Castle, Welshpool. The gist of the prophecy was that God was going to bring about a revival in Wales that was going to be profoundly based on unity amongst the Churches and it would last beyond the generation that first experienced it. I shared these and other prophecies given for Wales from America and South Korea at the Llangasty meeting.

Two other pieces of information were important in explaining why my spirit became so excited. First, research has shown that there are more denominations per capita in Wales than in any other nation. This fact speaks of division and dissension, the breaking down of relationships over issues such as church governance, doctrine, theology, and music. The answer as to why God has allowed such fragmentation of His Church may be found in the words of Jesus' prayer in John 17:20-24. Jesus prayed,

> *"My prayer is not for them alone. I pray also for those who will believe in me through their message, that all of them may be one, Father, just as you are in me and I am in you. May they also be in us so that the world may believe that you have sent me. I have given them the glory that you gave me that they may be one as we are one: I in them and you in me. May they be brought to complete unity to let the world know that you sent me and have loved them as you have loved me."*

It is clear here that Jesus is aware of the vital importance for unity amongst believers and the effectiveness of the proclamation of the gospel message. So where on earth might we find the greatest quality of unity amongst believers to which Jesus was referring? The answer could be in Wales. If God moved again in Wales and brought unity amongst the churches, the like of which had never been experienced before, then a dynamic transformation could result in which the effectiveness of the proclamation of the gospel would see greater numbers than ever being enfolded into the Church.

The second piece of information is that revivals typically last about seven years and then they fade away. These revivals are often named after an individual 'revivalist' or a single church. However, the prophecies mentioned above indicated powerfully what God was going to do in Wales wasn't to be based on an individual leader, but leaders, not in an individual Church, but Churches. There was a real sense at the meeting in Llangasty we were on the cusp of something that had the potential to be a significant part of the outworking of the prophetic words for our nation.

The leaders Bruce had gathered together continued to meet for over two years for prayer and discussion until *New Wine Cymru* had been formed and a leadership team established that met the criteria for the development of the accepted vision. Julian Richards, the co-leader with his wife Sarah of Cornerstone Church, Swansea, was appointed as the overall leader of *New Wine Cymru*.

During this period, I had the opportunity of going with a group of leaders to visit Bethel Church in Redding, California. Bill Johnson was the senior pastor of the church and he was attracting worldwide attention through his ministry and teaching. Our time there coincided with the Bethel School of Supernatural Ministry being delivered to over 800 delegates from nearly 50 countries. The 'School' lasts between one and three years and the intention is to train Christians to be involved in Revivalist ministry. We were able to attend some of the classes and also to be observers at one of their Leaders Meetings.

In that Bill Johnson had spent time with John Wimber to promote the Healing Ministry in the Church, I was particularly interested to discover new insights in the subject of Healing. I found the teaching to be both profound and biblical together with testimonies that often left me quite tearful.

As we entered the church and its grounds there was a tangible sense of the presence of God. I felt as if I was walking on holy ground. Some described this feeling as an entering into an open portal from heaven to earth. Faith soared and consequent belief in the miraculous seemed to be in the air that was breathed. In the grounds of the church was a small building that was open every day of the year for those wishing to be in total quietness, just to be in the presence of God with little or no agenda. The book of testimonies there was full of life changing stories and numerous healings. I spent most of our lunchtimes there just lying on the floor with a pillow for my head. Tears rolled down my face and all that I could say in my mind was, "Oh God, oh God." Without any articulation on my part, I sensed the Lord ministering His forgiveness, healing and anointing.

Bethel Church has this strap-line to describe itself:

We are a vibrant family of hope-filled believers who deeply experience the love and presence of God and partner with Jesus to express the joy and power of His Kingdom in every area of life.

We were privileged to experience something of the truth of these words in a memorable time spent together.

Bruce invited some of us to attend a national *New Wine* conference in Nottingham. There is no doubting the fact that there was a renewed sense of confidence and boldness in the Church to be able to proclaim the gospel in both word and deed.

During one lunchtime, I sat next to a lady who seemed both withdrawn and sad. She told me she and her husband had attended the conference even though her husband was dying with incurable cancer. His condition had deteriorated whilst they were there and he was in the accommodation they had rented, unable to get out of bed. As she told me her story, my faith rose and I knew I had to ask the lady if I could pray for her husband. She readily agreed. I asked one of the delegates if he wanted to see the Lord at work in healing. He appreciated the invitation and his faith was one of belief and expectancy.

When we arrived at the flat, her husband was still in bed. He was feverish and in some distress. We prayed for the Lord to heal him of the cancer and there were visible signs of improvement but not a complete healing. We encouraged the couple to be steadfast in their faith and gave them a prayer to pray for a continuation in his healing. When I didn't see the lady in the afternoon or evening session that day, I wondered what had happened. However, the following day I met her and was told the wonderful news that in the afternoon, the fever left him and the distension in his abdomen caused by the tumour had gone. He felt well enough to go with his wife for a long walk in a local park. Moments like these are quite wonderful and extremely encouraging.

Subsequent *New Wine Cymru* national conferences have recorded more denominational and non-denominational church strands coming together than ever before. The extent of the unity and love on these occasions is truly a work of God. Theological and doctrinal differences appear to have been put in their rightful context and value and not been a barrier to discovering the unity that Jesus prayed about in John 17:20-23. The temperature of unity and testimonies of healing are rising in our land and I believe this is a consequence of the prophecies previously mentioned being activated by the Lord in our day and age. We do not have a spiritual road map as to where this is all leading, but what we can be certain of is that this is the Lord's doing and we are responding to the Lord's calling and His plans for our nation.

We are greatly blessed to be given the privilege of being born in these days. Past generations have pined for times such as these, so it is up to us to press on and be a part of the advancement of the Kingdom of God on earth, with signs following, to the glory of God.

Healing, Heartache and Humour

29

And Finally...

I end this book with the testimony given by Jonathan on the day of his Confirmation Service. I believe this to be a source of encouragement for all those who are tempted to believe that experiences of the healing grace of God are reserved for the specially gifted Christians or for those who have been Church members for many years.

"Religion has never really played a big part in my life. I was the type of person who thought, that as long as I believed in God, I would be all right. I didn't think about God much.

"I suppose the change occurred when I got married to Sian. Sian is a Christian and has been since I've known her. On the rare occasions when I did attend church, I found that I did not enjoy some parts of it (especially Steve's sermons) and also, I found myself noticing the contentment of peoples' faces worshipping.

"My testimony starts on Monday October 1st, 2001. Steve was at my sister-in-law and brother-in-law's home. During the evening Steve gave his testimony. This impressed me greatly, and I found myself saying that I too wanted a personal experience of Jesus. To this Steve replied with a challenge, 'Come with me on Thursday to pray with a boy called Scott and I bet you will feel something. If you don't, I will hand my notice in on Sunday'. I couldn't believe what Steve was saying, putting his job on the line? What if I didn't feel anything? Christchurch would be without a vicar. Despite this predicament, I agreed to the challenge.

"Scott has a condition called R.S.D. He is in terrible pain. No one, even doctors, can touch certain parts of his body.

"Thursday October 4th, Steve picked me up and we went to Scott's house. Steve started praying and I laid my hands on Scott's knee. Within seconds I could feel his knee moving back and fore between my hands. There was also a pulsating motion coming from underneath his knee. During this time, I felt great warmth over my head, and my arms were shaking. The only way I can describe how my arms and hands felt is it's similar to when you hold out a heavy object in front of you for a long period of time. However, I was neither holding anything, nor did I have my arms outstretched, they were resting on the settee. After a short break, I then changed position and laid my hands on the underside of Scott's foot, again I felt a twitching movement back and fore underneath my hands.

"This night changed my life, thanks to Scott I have found and experienced Jesus. For the next four days I still had the tingling sensation going through my hands. I later found out that this is common when praying for healing.

"The following Tuesday which was October 9th, Sian and I started the *Alpha Course*. We had done the *Alpha Course* two years previous. The only reason why I had done it was because of Sian, and the only thing I got from it was meeting three great people, Alison John and Faith Wallbank, who I am proud to call friends.

"This *Alpha Course* started off differently, for one I wanted to do it and also I had my own experience of Jesus to give and share with others. I would recommend the *Alpha Course* to anyone who wants to find out more about Christianity and want to find answers to the questions of life. The course for me came to a climax on Saturday November 24th. This was the Holy Spirit Day of the course. Even though I had experienced the power of the Holy Spirit at Scott's, I had never prayed for the Holy Spirit. So I asked Steve and the other members of the group to pray for me. Whilst they were praying, my legs and arms started to shake. My eyes were closed and I could feel the fluttering. During the prayer,

Steve said that Jesus is going to speak to me and that my response will be, 'You've got to be joking'. It was also revealed that there was a clue in the meaning of my name, which happens to mean 'gift from God'.

"This is not the first time that I have stood up and given my testimony. Steve has asked me a couple of times to go with him to churches to speak. The first time was at a Methodist Church in Abercynon and the second was on Sunday November 25th at a church in Trethomas in Caerphilly. This church was alive, full of people on fire for Jesus. At the end of the service Steve asked people in the congregation that if there was anyone who wanted to receive Jesus as their saviour or prayer for healing they were to come to the front of the church. A lot of people unexpectedly came forward. Sian and I, and other members from Christchurch were beckoned forward to pray with these people. Sian and I were given a lady called Joyce. She was in her sixties and in a wheelchair. She tearfully told us that she had had a stroke two years previously and had been unable to walk since. We prayed with her. After a while, Sian started talking to Joyce and she explained the reason why she had cried. It wasn't because of her condition but that she no longer could do her work for Jesus. We then asked more specific questions about her illness and then prayed for her legs to be healed through Jesus' healing grace. I placed my hands on her knee. Whilst we prayed, I could feel her knee moving and twitching inside, and could see her calf shaking. Sian continued to talk with Joyce for some time.

"Meanwhile, Steve was circulating so I called him over. Steve, not knowing about her condition, asked if she would like to stand. She did so hesitantly with Steve closely standing in front of her. With support, she put one leg in front of the other. Growing in confidence, she asked Steve to stand at the side of her holding her hand to see if she could walk on her own. She did. She walked up the aisle and that was the last I saw of her."

Healing, Heartache and Humour

Epilogue

My intention is that this book proves to be a source of encouragement to many, and that it may serve as a precursor for the *Training Manual for the Church's Ministry Of Healing* that I have begun to write.

Having experienced the wonder of God's healing grace over a period of forty seven years, I have come to the conclusion that we are privileged to be living in an age in which there is an unprecedented 'move of God' on a global scale. I believe that the restoration of the ministry of healing has an important part to play as churches seek to present the Gospel afresh in a rich variety of contexts with power as well as words. In this respect, we are simply aligning ourselves with Saint Paul who wrote to the Corinthian Church,

> *My message and my preaching were not with wise and persuasive words, but with a demonstration of the Spirit's power, so that your faith might not rest on men's wisdom, but on God's power.*

> 1 Corinthians 2:4-5

The commonly used phrase 'action speaks louder than words' is a well-used secular expression that correlates to the biblical injunction given to us by our Lord and Saviour, Jesus Christ. When Jesus sent out His disciples He said,

> *As you go, preach the message, 'the kingdom of heaven is near.' Heal the sick, raise the dead, cleanse those who have leprosy, drive out demons. Freely you have received, freely give.*

> Matthew 10:7-8

Mark's gospel records the result of this commissioning, *"They went out and preached that people should repent. They drove out many demons and anointed many sick people with oil and healed them"*.

I confess that the part of this commissioning given by Jesus to His disciples I have found most difficult is that of ministering to people who have demons. For a short while, I was comfortable with the notion what was diagnosed as 'demonic' in the times of Jesus could in these days be regarded as psychological or psychiatric aberrations. However, it was not long before I was disenfranchised from this opinion and I would like to explore this more fully in a chapter of my training manual. A number of people have come to me suffering from spiritual damage as a result of exorcism ministry that was either not necessary or simply done very badly.

The identifying and training a team of church members for healing ministry is an important part of the public and private presentation of the Church's mission to those who are not yet a part of the Church as well as its own members. Consequently, the need for teaching aids comes sharply into focus.

I cannot express what a joy it is to see human brokenness in all its forms being presented to Jesus and to see His love, mercy and power meet the needs and transform lives.

To play a small part in the equipping of churches and individuals for healing ministry is at the same time both humbling and an immense privilege.

#0044 - 301018 - C0 - 210/142/13 - PB - 9781907929908